W9-BTZ-023

CHRISTIAN UNITY

How *you* can make
a *difference*

THOMAS RYAN, CSP

Paulist Press
New York / Mahwah, NJ

Cover image credits: "Hand cross" by Colorscurves/Dreamstime.com; "Stained glass window" by Nanoya/Dreamstime.com
Cover design by Tamian Wood
Book design by Lynn Else

Library of Congress Cataloging-in-Publication Data

Ryan, Thomas, 1946-
    Christian unity : how you can make a difference / Thomas Ryan, CSP.
       pages cm
    Includes bibliographical references.
    ISBN 978-0-8091-4950-6 (pbk.) — ISBN 978-1-58768-549-1 (e-book)
    1. Ecumenical movement. 2. Catholic Church—Relations. 3. Church—Unity.
I. Title.
    BX1785.R895 2015
    280`.042—dc23

                                                                2015010700

ISBN 978-0-8091-4950-6 (paperback)
ISBN 978-1-58768-549-1 (e-book)

Published by Paulist Press
997 Macarthur Boulevard
Mahwah, New Jersey 07430

www.paulistpress.com

Printed and bound in the
United States of America

To two pioneers who led the way, Rev. Thomas Stransky, CSP,
and Rev. Irénée Beaubien, SJ, whose presence and wisdom
still bless us, and in grateful, loving memory of Rev. Jack Hotchkin,
Dr. Margaret O'Gara, and Brother Jeffrey Gros, FSC,
whose friendship, scholarship, and commitment provided
inspiration for the journey toward an increasingly visible
and missional unity among Christians.

CONTENTS

ACKNOWLEDGMENTS

This book, like the work for Christian unity, is the result of collaborative effort, of people sharing their stories and experiences and thereby making tangible and real a vital dimension of the church's mission that tends to be remote and abstract for many. I am very grateful to Fr. Joe Scott, CSP; Ray and Fenella Temmerman; Anne Marie and Norman Hicks; Dr. Mitzi Budde; Rev. Dr. Larry Golemon; Margaret O'Donnell; Don Krahmer, Jr., and other members of the Brothers in Christ network who have shared their personal experience, insights, and wisdom in these pages. And I offer a special word of thanks to my editor, Paul McMahon, with whom it has truly been a pleasure to work.

INTRODUCTION

There is much talk in these times about the new evangelization, about bringing the good news of Jesus into every human situation for the transformation of individual lives as well as society by the divine power of the gospel itself. And there's no question about it that in the midst of our war-torn and divided world, the core of the gospel is indeed good news: We are reconciled to God and to one another through the life, death, and resurrection of Jesus!

How can that message have any semblance of credibility when we Christians who bring it are divided amongst ourselves?

Every coin has two sides and the coin of the church's mission is no different. On one side is evangelization; on the other side is the work for Christian unity. The credibility of the message brought on one side of the coin requires, on the other side, that those who bring it are walking their talk. It is impossible for a coin to have only one side.

Not surprisingly, one of the two reasons why the Second Vatican Council was convened was the promotion of unity among Christians. The underlying conviction was that the church is to be a sign in the midst of the human community of God's intended wholeness for both church and world. For the first twenty-five years following the Council, there was a fresh and strong wind in the sails of efforts for an increasingly visible unity and solidarity among the followers of Jesus. In the last twenty-five, however, the wind seems to have died down with a resulting diminution of forward movement in the boat.

The reasons are varied. It's taking longer than anticipated. As old disagreements were resolved, new ones have surfaced. People have only so much time and energy, and they want to see the results of their efforts in their lifetimes. Our contemporary culture tends to make a positive virtue of diversity.

Consequently, living in an increasingly religiously plural society, energy has shifted to a new field of encounter—relations with followers of other world religions—that is not only important in its own right, but is more exotic and intriguing and where the bar is not raised as high. Mutual understanding, respect, collaboration in meeting the challenges we commonly face in our society is more easily attainable than the intra-Christian goal of unity in faith, life, worship, and mission.

While that may be so, it does not release Christians from taking the other side of the coin seriously, with steadfast commitment to it. Having already addressed the mutual richness of the interreligious (to be distinguished from ecumenical) encounter in four earlier books,[1] the focus in this book is on our responsibility, in obedience to the prayer of Jesus (John 17:21), to be actively involved in deepening and rendering more visible our bonds of unity with one another as Christians.

Do we still—did we ever—feel the pain of the divisions within the one Body of Christ? Have we adapted to it or just come to accept it as "the way things are"? If the latter is the case, and many Christians today do feel no pain at this profoundly abnormal situation, then the seemingly present disposition to settle simply for occasional cooperation is understandable. If so, we are making peace with *not* being the church God wills.

It is time to relight the fire at the grassroots and to remind ourselves that the ecumenical movement began as a lay undertaking in Bible societies, missionary fields, the Student Christian Movement, and in associations like the YMCA and the YWCA, and in lay uprisings against the stultifying fragmentation of the church.

The pattern, however, is for new, exciting movements to become institutionalized and, in so doing, risk losing the popular and large-scale grassroots support that gave them such momentum in the first place. This has happened to the ecumenical movement to a very real extent. It has by and large gone from living room dialogues to formally appointed officers, commissions, conferences, and high-level dialogues. While it is wonderful to have such institutional support to keep a movement going in good times and in bad, without ongoing grassroots interest and support, the wind will die down and the boat will fail to reach its destination.

The cry must go out: "All hands on deck! Grab the oars and start paddling!" What church members in general must realize is that while those at the official levels play an important part in keeping the momentum going, they cannot do it alone. We all are part of the crew and have important, albeit different, roles to play. The chapters of this book seek to provide a clearer sense of the contribution each of us can make.

Whether you are a pastor or a parish member, an interchurch couple or family, a member of a religious community or lay movement, a student or professor, a social action group or a network of community leaders in society, *you can make a difference.*

Therefore, the first two chapters will examine the spiritual and theological foundations of ecumenism—the "why?" and the "what?"—that are required for staying the course. We will then look closely in the ensuing chapters at a broad range of grassroots possibilities for the engagement of laity and clergy alike at local levels. These are by and large the "action" chapters, sprinkled generously with inspiring personal stories and interviews that bring things from the cerebral to the concrete. They provide a very down-to-earth picture of the different forms that being an active agent for reconciliation in the Body of Christ can take.

So, if your tendency has been to regard Christian unity as too airy-fairy or one of those things that'll never happen with the resulting thought, "I'm not going to give *that* any of my time or energy," the content of these pages will invite you to think again and, I hope, motivate you to action.

Our gospel mission is to make the church we know and to which we belong a sign of wholeness and reconciliation in the midst of our local communities and in the human family. Yes, it is indeed a big project because it's a *God project.* And each one of us can make a positive contribution to it if our eyes, ears, minds, and hearts are open to the possibilities before us in the little world within which we live and move.

1. WHAT JESUS DESIRES FOR US

OK, so you grew up and went to school with kids who went to other churches in your neighborhood or town or city suburb. Maybe you played either with them or against them on the soccer field or basketball court or baseball diamond. Or maybe you sang in choir together or went to the prom together or had tandem roles in the senior class play. However, you didn't talk much about your faith together.

Then came—or comes, if that's the life stage you're presently in—your job, home, marriage, and family. Friends and acquaintances, as well as those you've never met, continue to find their way to a church down the block or around the corner, and you politely wave to one another as you pass en route to your respective congregations. There's respect for each other's upbringing and/or personal choices, but the faith dimension of your lives is not something that you've ever or often focused on or discussed with one another in any depth. It remains a personal, family thing. The name of the game is politeness, respect, discretion—like two people working in the kitchen at preparing a meal without communicating with each other.

Does this situation even begin to approach God's dream for us? God longs to build us together into a family where the communication among us is so heartfelt and the love among us is so tangible that it makes outsiders long to discover God and join us. This kingdom construction project is essentially about God's desire to construct a new community animated by love and collaboration. So it's much more about breaking down every dividing wall between us than about us politely smiling at and bypassing one another. To that end,

God asks us to set aside our ignorance, indifference, and prejudices so that we can treasure one another and learn from one another. Together we have the opportunity to express God's multifaceted love to the world, and to do so far more powerfully than any one church could ever do alone.

Unity among Christians is thus both a gift and a task. As a gift, unity is given to us in Christ through our common baptism. It's not something we invent from our own resources. God creates it, but we have a certain responsibility in living it, in making it visible to the world for the advance of God's reign in the world. It's a gift that's meant to be used for more effective mission, not carried quietly and discretely or put in a closet and forgotten.

Certainly, working for Christian unity today feels like running uphill. Or it may seem like a style of dress that was popular thirty years ago but isn't seen much today. For some, given their church community's clergy shortage or financial constraints, investing time and energy or material resources in the work for Christian unity feels more like a luxury than a necessity. If it takes the form of a project that could actually *save* money, it might have a better chance (note that pragmatism, not unity, is the prime value here). But unity among the followers of Jesus is not to be sought because it would further some other cause.

The division of the church, the inability of those who recognize one another as Christians to *live* a common life in Christ, is in itself something the whole church is called to overcome. Overcoming that self-contradiction is an important and necessary task. Let's examine some of the foundational reasons that should motivate us to keep taking the next step, no matter how small.

1. THE PRAYER OF JESUS

Imagine that you had the opportunity to spend the last hours with someone who has had a powerful influence on your life, someone whose teaching and mentoring has shaped your sense of self and defined your attitudes to others and to the world at large.

There you are, by the side of his or her bed, hoping and expecting that he or she will dig down deep and come up with the distilled

wisdom of a lifetime to leave with you as a kind of summary statement of what really matters in life.

Such is the situation of the apostles with Jesus at the Last Supper.
He only has a few hours left with them and he knows it. It is a special
time, and the particular message he wants to leave with them has the
character of a last will and testament. What does he say?

> And now I am no longer in the world, but they are in the
> world, and I am coming to you. Holy Father, protect them
> in your name that you have given me, so that they may be
> one, as we are one....I ask you to protect them from the
> evil one....I ask not only on behalf of these, but also on
> behalf of those who will believe in me through their word,
> that they may all be one. As you, Father, are in me and I
> am in you, may they also be in us, so that the world may
> believe that you have sent me. The glory that you have
> given me I have given them, so that they may be one, as
> we are one. (John 17:11, 15, 20–22)

Four times in this one prayer, Jesus prays that those who follow him
and those who come to believe in him through their witness may live
in unity with one another. Furthermore, he prays for our protection
from "the evil one," the *devil*, a name that in Greek (*diabolos*) means
"one who divides." The work of the diabolical one is to bring division, to divide people from God as well as from one another. The evil
one seeks especially to bring division to those who have been gifted
with the trinitarian unity shared by God through Jesus and in the
Holy Spirit.

Given the timing and the framework in which that message
comes to us, there is no dodging its centrality in Jesus' priorities for
his followers. The values at the heart of Jesus' own living and prayer
set the agenda for the mission of the church today.

On another occasion, while Jesus was engaged in talking with a
gathering of people at Peter's house, someone approached him and
told him his mother and family were outside, asking for him. And his
response is, "Who are my mother and my brothers?" Then he answers
his own question by saying, "Whoever does the will of God is my
brother and sister and mother" (Mark 3:33, 35).

In a society where blood relationship meant everything, this statement is a stunning one. Blood may be thicker than water but, Jesus asserts, faith is thicker than blood. Faith trumps biology as the real basis for family. So we need to radiate Jesus' hunger for solidarity with people of sincere faith in all denominations who strive to hear the word of God and keep it. Our actions toward them should be marked by respect, graciousness, and charity, but we should also let them know that we long for more visible unity with them. None of us has arrived. As individuals and as churches, our primary task is to be more faithful to the gospel. The closer we come to Jesus, the closer we will come to one another.[1]

2. THE TEACHING OF THE APOSTLES

The theme of Jesus' Last Supper prayer for the unity of his followers is picked up by his closest circle and expressed in a variety of images. Paul's Letters to the Corinthians, Romans, and the Ephesians bear some sterling examples:

> Now I appeal to you, brothers and sisters, by the name of our Lord Jesus Christ, that all of you be in agreement and that there be no divisions among you, but that you be united in the same mind and the same purpose. (1 Cor 1:10)

> For just as the body is one and has many members, and all the members of the body, though many, are one body, so it is with Christ….Now you are the body of Christ and individually members of it. (1 Cor 12:12, 27)

> For as in one body we have many members, and not all the members have the same function, so we, who are many, are one body in Christ, and individually we are members one of another. (Rom 12:4–5)

We might hear in these calls the words that Augustine liked to say in holding up the bread and cup before distributing holy communion: "Receive what you are, and be to one another what you receive."

In the first three chapters of Paul's Letter to the Ephesians, he relates God's saving work for the whole world through the cross of Christ, reconciling a divided humanity into one body. In the ensuing chapters, Paul moves into identifying the concrete practices and behaviors that will give visible expression to a now-reconciled humanity:

> I therefore, the prisoner in the Lord, beg you to lead a life worthy of the calling to which you have been called, with all humility and gentleness, with patience, bearing with one another in love, making every effort to maintain the unity of the Spirit in the bond of peace. There is one body and one Spirit, just as you were called to the one hope of your calling, one Lord, one faith, one baptism, one God and Father of all, who is above all and through all and in all. (Eph 4:1–6)

He doesn't say, "Create some unity among yourselves." He says, "*Maintain* the unity." Safeguard it. Protect it. Defend it. God has already given it to you. Hold on to it and keep it from harm.

Alas, the Body of Christ is already wounded. Some of those wounds have already been there a long time, inflicted by other churches on our own church centuries ago. Other wounds have been inflicted more recently by fellow members of our own denomination in the strife that is taking place within and that has weakened if not torn apart many church bodies today. It would be easy to just go our separate ways and distance ourselves from those fomenting the current divisions, but in light of Jesus' prayer for the unity of his followers and the teachings of the apostles, going that route is not an option.[2]

The Ecumenical Directory of the Catholic Church states, "No Christian should be satisfied with these forms of communion. They do not correspond to the will of Christ and weaken his church in its mission." (no. 19)[3]

Faithful to the biblical mandate expressed above, the World Council of Churches states that the goal of the ecumenical movement is "to call the churches to the goal of visible unity in one faith and one eucharistic fellowship expressed in worship and in common life in Christ, and to advance to that unity in order that the world may believe."[4]

3. THE CREDIBILITY OF THE GOSPEL

If we had to distill the message of the gospel into one quintessential statement, mine would be the following: We are reconciled to God and to one another through the life, death, and resurrection of Jesus. And the primary mission of the church is to carry that message out to the world. Ask any missionary, however, what happens when you try to bring the good news of reconciliation to those outside the church. In effect, what comes back is this: "Well, I hear what you're saying—'We're reconciled to God and to one another'—but I also see what you *are*: divided amongst yourselves. Your 'good news' lacks credibility."

How much damage to the credibility of the gospel can be sustained before unity becomes a key priority for the churches?

At the opening service for the Second World Conference on Faith and Order in Edinburgh, Scotland, in 1937, one of the great Christian leaders of the century, Archbishop of Canterbury and theologian William Temple, preached a powerful sermon in which he likened divisions among Christians to a dark veil hanging over a light.

> It is as though a lantern were covered with a dark veil. It is truly a lantern, because the light burns in it; yet the world sees the light but dimly and may be more conscious of the veil that hides it than of the flame which is its source. So the world may see the sin of Christians more clearly than the holiness of the Church, and the divisions which that sin has caused more clearly than the unity which endures in spite of them.
>
> When that happens, and in whatever degree it happens, the witness of the Church is weakened. How can it call men to worship of the one God if it is calling to rival shrines? How can it claim to bridge the divisions in human society…if when men are drawn into it they find that another division has been added to the old ones—a

division of Catholic from Evangelical, or Episcopalian from Presbyterian or Independent? A Church divided in its manifestation to the world cannot render its due service to God or to man, and, for the impotence which our sin has brought upon the Church through divisions in its outward aspect; we should be covered with shame and driven to repentance.

To Him, the Conqueror of death and sin—to Him, the Lamb of God who taketh away the sin of the world—we call the world that its sins may be removed, that its divisions may be healed, and that it may find fellowship in Him.

That proclamation, that invitation, we are bound as a Church to make. And the world answers: "Have you found that fellowship yourselves? Why do your voices sound so various? When we pass from words to action, to what are you calling us? Is it to one family, gathered round one Holy Table, where your Lord is Himself the host who welcomes all His guests? You know that it is not so. When we answer your united call, we have to choose for ourselves to which Table we will go, for you are yourselves divided in your act of deepest fellowship, and by your own traditions hinder us from a unity which we are ready to enjoy."

God grant that we may feel the pain of it, and under that impulsion strive the more earnestly to remove all that now hinders us from receiving together the One Body of the One Lord, that in Him we may become One Body—the organ and vehicle of the One Spirit.

If it is true that in its deepest nature the Church is always one, it is also true that today it is the so-called "churches" rather than any forces of the secular world which prevent that unity from being manifest and effective.[5]

The church is in mission through what it *is*, not just through what it says and does. The division among Christians—our failure to live out the common life in Christ we believe the Lord calls us to—is something the church as a whole is called to overcome. In some sense, we believe that we make up the one Body, but we cannot now live a common life. A divided church, not just a church with distinct traditions or distinct organizations, but a church that cannot cele‐ brate one Eucharist or hold a universal council to settle a pressing question, is a church living in self-contradiction. Seeking to over‐ come that self-contradiction is a necessary task for the credibility of the gospel we teach and seek to share with others.

Thus did the bishops gathered from around the world at the Second Vatican Council say, "The restoration of unity among all Christians is one of the principal concerns of the Second Vatican Council....Certainly, such division openly contradicts the will of Christ, scandalizes the world, and damages that most holy cause, the preaching of the gospel to every creature" (Decree on Ecumenism 1).[6]

The credibility of the gospel depends upon the unity of the church by which the life-in-communion of the triune God is to be exhibited to the world. In other words, the unity of the church is a necessary condition for holding the gospel true.

4. THE VOCATION OF THE CHURCH: MISSION

There is an inherent and unbreakable connection between mis‐ sion and unity. In its recent convergence statement, *The Church: Towards a Common Vision*, the World Council of Churches' Faith and Order Commission describes that connection:

> The Church, as the body of Christ, acts by the power of the Holy Spirit to continue his life-giving mission in prophetic and compassionate ministry and so participate in God's work of healing a broken world. Communion, whose source is the very life of the Holy Trinity, is both the gift by which the Church lives and, at the same time, the gift that God calls the Church to offer to a wounded and divided humanity in hope of reconciliation and healing.
>
> As a divinely established communion, the Church belongs to God and does not exist for itself. It is by its very nature missionary, called and sent to witness in its own

life to that communion which God intends for all humanity and for all creation in the kingdom.[7]

One of the scriptural citations that we are not accustomed to hearing related to Christian unity but that profoundly makes the connection between unity and mission is Jesus' teaching about the Good
Shepherd:

> I am the good shepherd. The good shepherd lays down his
> life for the sheep....I know my own and my own know me,
> just as the Father knows me and I know the Father. And
> I lay down my life for the sheep. I have other sheep that
> do not belong to this fold. I must bring them also, and
> they will listen to my voice. So there will be one flock,
> one shepherd. (John 10:11, 14–16)

In earlier verses (2, 7, and 9), we hear that there is one gate,
one flock, and one shepherd. What the Good Shepherd wants is to
have all the sheep together in one flock, enclosed in one sheepfold.
And for this, he is ready to die to gather the sheep, but the purpose
of his death will not be completely fulfilled until they are one. The
Shepherd's mission is to unite. And just as mission and unity are twin
imperatives for Jesus—he is portrayed as coming to unite and dying
to make one—so also are they two sides of a coin for his church. For
the church's mission to be effective in carrying out his command "to
go into the world and preach the gospel to every creature," the members of his Body, the church, will have to be united with one another
in that mission. If it is not a unity the world can see, then it falls
short of the unity for which Jesus prayed.[8]

The ultimate purpose of Christian unity is mission-oriented: "so
that the world may believe that you have sent me." Visible unity is a
critical dimension of our witness. When, as a result of our divisions,
we are not yet united at the Lord's Table and not yet able to bring
prophetic witness together in the face of injustice, our witness is
compromised and drained of its compelling power.

The church has a job to do in the world. In its tasks of pro-
claiming the gospel, promoting social justice, and peacemaking, one
might say that the world is too strong for a divided church. The problems are too vast and too deep for piecemeal responses.

The Catholic Church's *Directory for the Application of Principles and Norms on Ecumenism* puts it strongly:

> No Christian should be satisfied with these present forms of partial communion. They do not correspond to the will of Christ, and weaken his church in the exercise of its mission. The grace of God has impelled members of many churches and ecclesial communities, especially in the course of this present century, to strive to overcome the divisions inherited from the past and to build anew a communion of love by prayer, by repentance and by asking pardon of each other for sins of disunity past and present, by meeting in practical forms of cooperation and in theological dialogue. These are the aims and activities of what has come to be called the ecumenical movement. (no. 19)

The understanding of the nature of the church that is coming into broad acceptance through the ecumenical dialogues is that the church is called to be a Communion of communions. Thus, full visible unity among all the baptized—so that the churches may truly become a sign of that full communion in the one, holy, catholic, and apostolic church of Jesus Christ—is not a take-it-or-leave-it proposition. Every Christian is called upon to be an active agent of unity with other members of the Body of Christ. In its Decree on Ecumenism, the Second Vatican Council declared that "concern for restoring unity pertains to the whole Church, faithful and clergy alike. It extends to everyone, according to the potential of each" (no. 4).

If any church member still felt inclined to relate to the church's mission for unity with indifference or an attitude of leaving it up to others, Pope John Paul II removed the wiggle room when in his encyclical, On Commitment to Ecumenism, he said "the way of ecumenism is the way of the Church" (no. 7), and then went on to underline that statement further with these words: "Thus it is absolutely clear that ecumenism, the movement promoting Christian Unity, is not just some sort of appendix which is added to the Church's traditional activity. Rather, ecumenism is an organic part of her life and work, and consequently must pervade all she is and does" (no. 20).[9]

When he was president of the Pontifical Council for Promoting Christian Unity, Edward Idris Cardinal Cassidy put it this way in a lecture given in Rome on "The Principles of Ecumenism":

> We Christians have not chosen one another; we have been chosen. And because it is the one Christ who has done the choosing, we have been chosen to be his together. Unity is not then our choice. Ecumenism is not optional. Ecumenism is not our effort to achieve a unity that does not exist. Rather it is our response to the gift of unity already given. Like it or not, the gift and the problems that come with the gift, are already ours.[10]

From the beginning, evangelization and ecumenism have been like twins. Neither is an end in itself. Each is the will of the Lord and a gift of the Spirit. Together, they represent the historical dynamism of the church of Christ that, in line with God's salvific design, gathers people from all parts of the earth into one family of faith. Together, evangelization and ecumenism are the path of the church toward the future.

5. OUR MODEL OF UNITY IN DIVERSITY: THE TRINITY

Orthodox bishop Kallistos Ware of Oxford gave a talk in Pittsburgh about the relationship between Orthodox and Eastern Catholics. He began by asking the following question: "Why should I care about Christian unity?" And his answer was, "I care about Christian unity because I believe in the Holy Trinity." The bishop then drew out the implications of our trinitarian faith: our God is not a monad who lives in splendid isolation, but a triad of Father, Son, and Holy Spirit, loving one another from all eternity. This means that, in the deepest depths of the divine mystery, God is a relational being. And if we humans are made in the image and likeness of God, if we are images, living icons of God the Trinity, then we too are relational beings. We most perfectly image the Trinity when we too love one another in a selfless way. We are saved not in isolation from one another, but within the complex web of relationships that make up the Christian community. In the eastern rite liturgy of St. John Chrysostom, there is the prayer "Let us love one another *so that* we may confess Father, Son, and Holy Spirit."[11]

So the upshot of this, observed Fr. Ronald Roberson, CSP, is that

> if we do not love one another, if we don't make it our concern to break down misunderstanding and division, we are a poor image of the Trinity, and we cannot give authentic praise to God. That is why Christians must be concerned about reconciliation, about overcoming the misunderstandings and divisions that prevent us from offering a more perfect image of the Trinity to our broken world. It is simply not acceptable to say that those other people are wrong and we are right. We have to do more to break down the barriers, to recognize our own shortcomings, to reach out to others in love, especially and above all to our fellow baptized Christians. That is why Pope John Paul said in his encyclical *That All May Be One*,[12] that the way of ecumenism is the way of the Church. "Unity," he wrote, is not "some secondary attribute of the community of [Christ's] disciples. Rather, it belongs to the very essence of this community."[13]

The Trinity is life in community, a community made up of persons with diverse gifts and missions, all of whom love, honor, and respect one another. And the source of the church's unity is nothing less than the unifying life of the one God who dwells in us and makes us one. The unity of the shared life and work of the three persons of the Trinity is the model for our life together in the church. The lives of churches in relationship to other churches and the lives of individual church members ought to be as inseparably interrelated as the three interlocking circles that symbolize the Trinity.

The Trinity is not only a model for the church in terms of unity in diversity, but in terms of the great biblical theme of sending and gathering as well. There is triune action in the sending. The Father sends the Son into the world out of love for the world. The Father and the Son together send the Holy Spirit upon the church to empower its mission. And the risen Christ, after endowing his disciples with the

Holy Spirit, sends them into the world on behalf of the Father. Once you ground the sending of the church in the triune nature of God, the idea of mission is infused with that of unity.

Similarly, there is a triune action in the movement of gathering. The Father seeks to gather up all things in Christ, as the Good Shepherd gathers his sheep. Jesus was, in short, *sent* to *gather*. We cannot speak of one without the other. However, there is more: it is the Holy Spirit who enables believers to gather together and experience the reality of their unity. These two movements of the mission of God—sending and gathering—are intimately grounded and interconnected in the trinitarian action of God, thereby infusing the very idea of mission with the characteristic of unity. In the end, the mission of God in the world must lead to unity because it flows from unity.[14]

In a homily given in Istanbul during his apostolic journey to Turkey, Pope Francis underlined the role of the Holy Spirit:

> The Holy Spirit is the soul of the Church. He *gives life*, he *brings forth different charisms* which enrich the people of God and, above all, he *creates unity* among believers: from the many he makes one body, the Body of Christ. The Church's whole life and mission depend on the Holy Spirit; he fulfills all things.
>
> In our journey of faith and fraternal living, the more we allow ourselves to be humbly guided by the Spirit of the Lord, the more we will overcome misunderstandings, divisions, and disagreements and be a credible sign of unity and peace, a credible sign that our Lord is risen and he is alive.[15]

UNITY AND MISSION IN THE TWENTY-FIRST CENTURY

Most of us who have grown up in our divided churches unconsciously assume that this is the normal situation. Ecumenism or the work for unity among the followers of Jesus then becomes abnormal. However, the fact that we Christians have lived for centuries with our divisions does not make these phenomena *normal*, even though they may be widely accepted and *familiar*. So let's not confuse *familiar* with *normal*. The unfortunate fact is that we are reasonably comfortable with the way things are and we feel very virtuous if we take a few tentative steps toward infrequent collaboration with other Christians. The abnormality of followers of Jesus living out of communion with one another is largely lost upon us. Where the division of the one Body of Christ is no longer perceived as an offense and no longer causes pain, ecumenism becomes superfluous. A group of sixteen theologians from various church traditions said it well in the Princeton Proposal for Christian Unity:

> Where division is regarded as normal, is no longer perceived as a scandal and a wound, the gift of unity that is the "mystery of God's will," his "plan for the fullness of time" (Ephesians 1:9–10) will remain hidden by human ignorance and sin. To work towards the real and concrete growth of unity among all our churches is, we believe, an imperative for the conscience of every Christian."
>
> The Church is by its very nature missionary, called and sent to witness in its own life to that communion which God intends for all humanity. A common life, in which those who were divided are reconciled in the body of Christ, is an essential goal of the mission that God has appointed for us. God gathers those who comprise the Church in order to bring unity to a divided humanity. If we accept division among ourselves as Christians as normal and inevitable, we turn away from the mission God has given us.
>
> Friendly division is still division. We must not let our present division be seen as normal, as the natural expression of a Christian marketplace with churches representing different options for a variety of spiritual tastes. Consumerist values and an ideology of diversity can anesthetise us to the wound of division. Recovering from this ecumenical anesthesia is one of the strongest present challenges to faithfulness.[16]

In a talk at The Catholic University of America, Cardinal Kurt Koch, the president of the Pontifical Council for Promoting Christian Unity, asked whether we Christians do in fact still feel the painful offense of the division of the one Body of Christ, or whether we have over time adapted to it or even come to terms with it. We will only uncover new energy for Christian unity efforts, he said, when we have the courage and the humility to look this abiding offense in the face.

> That Christians who believe in Jesus Christ as the Redeemer of the world and are baptized into his one body continue to live in churches separated from one another, is the great offence which Christendom still offers to the world today and which deserves to be called a scandal. This does not only consist in the fact that we cannot yet celebrate the eucharist together, but even more fundamentally in the fact that we as churches continue to be separated and as Christendom continue to be divided. To overcome this offence must remain the aim of ecumenical activity. Church divisions are in any case to be identified as the division of that which is essentially indivisible, namely the unity of the body of Christ.[17]

Koch went on to observe how, in the passion narrative, when the Roman soldiers proceeded to strip Jesus of his robe, described in Scripture as "seamless, woven in one piece" (John 19:23), they did not dare to cut up this precious garment, saying, "Let us not tear it" (19:24). In Christian history, that robe of Jesus has served as a symbol of the unity of the church as the Body of Christ. The terrible tragedy of this story, he said, consists in the fact that Christians themselves have done what the Roman soldiers did not dare to do. And thus today, the robe of Christ appears "in rags and tatters, in confessions and denominations which have often battled against one another throughout history instead of fulfilling their Lord's mandate that they be one."[18]

Christians have an incredible message to get out, but our speech is defective, and what we want to say is not the message the world hears. It's frustrating for God and it's frustrating for us, the church. Furthermore, it's a tragedy for the world, which desperately wants and needs to hear some genuinely "good news."

In the stretch of sea ahead, we need a missional approach that holistically integrates unity and mission, affirming that they are bound together in the purposes of God. Effective mission requires both diversity and unity. The gospel must be brought into different cultural contexts with sensitivity to and respect for each. But while mission thus creates diversity, it also demands unity so that the diversity remains rooted in the one gospel. And the unity referred to here is not so much expressed in an additional set of activities like interchurch meetings; rather, it is expressed in the core activities of the church of Christ such as worshipping, witnessing, and serving. Unity is not about doing extra "ecumenical things," but about doing what we're already doing ecumenically. If we take this angle of approach in our compass bearings, we will not see evangelization, social justice, and church unity as conflicting concerns but as complementary aspects of the one mission of God as we engage in them *together*.[19]

Pope Francis, who has welcomed several groups of evangelical and other Christians to private meetings in his residence, said he senses a widespread and strong desire for full Christian unity. When the Pontifical Council for Promoting Christian Unity was holding its plenary meeting and celebrating the fiftieth anniversary of the Second Vatican Council's Decree on Ecumenism, Pope Francis gave them a text in which he wrote, "I am convinced of this: In a common journey, under the guidance of the Holy Spirit and learning from one another, we can grow in the communion that already unites us....The search for full unity of Christians remains a priority for the Catholic Church and, therefore, it is one of my principal daily preoccupations."[20]

The Canadian Conference of Catholic Bishops marked the Decree's fiftieth anniversary with an extraordinarily rich document titled "A Church in Dialogue: Towards the Restoration of Unity Among Christians." This document acknowledges that we live in a period of real but incomplete transition, and that we need to find a way to live deeply and faithfully in the midst of it, filling that period with real life:

> The churches did not only diverge through discussion, they diverged through the way they lived, through alienation

and estrangement. Therefore, they need to come closer to each other again in their lives; they must get accustomed to each other, to pray together, work together, live together.

A dialogue of life compels us, as appropriate, to move out of our separate compartments, to learn to live our Christian life and mission together. The fact is, Christian communities do not "do everything together that is allowed by their faith"; it is indeed more the case that we act separately except where extraordinary circumstances move us to act together. There is much room for growth here. While we continue to feel the sting of our incomplete communion and of restrictions that keep us from *eucharistic* communion around the Lord's table, there is much more that we can do together. Furthermore, doing what we can do together will deepen our desire for full visible unity and our commitment "to build anew a communion of love" (Ecumenical Directory, 19; cf. Decree on Ecumenism, 12).[21]

The bishops encourage church members to exercise in equal measure the twin virtues of ecumenism—patience and perseverance—without glossing over difficulties and showing genuine commitment in the quest, motivated by the urgent need for reconciliation and by Christ's own desire for the unity of his disciples.

The church has a mission in the world: to be a sacrament, a visible sign of God's already present reign, both to bring the message and to be a test case for it; to live in such a way among ourselves as Christians that the message of reconciliation we bring can be read by anyone who cares to look at our own relationships among ourselves.

The foundation of common mission is the recognition that we have been given that mission by the Lord, and he has commissioned us to carry it out together as his Body in the world. Such collaboration expresses the bond that already unites us and is itself a form of proclamation and a manifestation of Christ himself.[22]

It's no use walking somewhere to preach unless you're preaching as you walk. Or as Tradition holds, Francis of Assisi put it thus:

"Preach the gospel wherever you go. If necessary, use words." Are we walking our talk? Living our message?

Every member of the church, each according to his or her talents and abilities, has a role to play in helping congregational members grow in unity with other Christians, avoiding expressions, judgments, and actions that are not truthful or misrepresent their faith and practice. We are all encouraged to exercise initiative and to take an active and intelligent part in the work of promoting Christian unity.[23]

Why is it important that Christians seize every opportunity to visibly manifest our unity? Why did Jesus desire it and pray for it? Because the church we are called to be is the community of those who, because of Christ, are no longer separated. It is a contradiction to speak of "separated Christians." Reconciliation, unity, is of the very nature of the church of Christ. This is the direct link between the church's mission for unity and its mission to evangelize: unity is *for* more effective mission.

2. WHAT DO WE MEAN BY "UNITY"?

A good metaphor for the efforts of the last half century on behalf of Christian unity is a plane journey. After long and careful preparation, the plane revs up its engines and quickly builds up speed as it heads down the runway, soon taking off into a steep upward climb. Once it reaches cruising altitude and levels off, the stimulation provided by the upward thrust fades to the point that it hardly feels like one is moving at all, or at most, very slowly. Especially in international flights, those in window seats are presented with a marvelous panorama—the ecumenical activity of the past fifty years—and they receive the benefit of illuminating perspectives that allow them to appreciate the great diversity of Christianity in the world today. In the course of this long ecumenical plane journey, one can become so accustomed to the cruising altitude that the destination of the journey risks becoming a blur on the horizon.[1]

What *is* our destination on this journey for Christian unity? What do we mean by *unity*? Other metaphors relative to the official ecumenical movement certainly abound today in phrases like *the winter of ecumenism* or *a stagnant pond*. Some fifty years of dialogue have resulted in an institutional or doctrinal fatigue, with finely crafted statements but little real progress to show for it in terms of realities on the ground. A good example of this is the historic agreement between Lutherans and Catholics worldwide on the issue at the heart of the sixteenth-century Protestant Reformation: How are we saved? Is it by faith or by works? Yet one could ask, in spite of that 1999 Declaration on the Doctrine of Justification between the Lutheran World Federation and the Catholic Church, are Lutherans and Catholics now relating to one another differently in any significant ways? Is peaceful coexistence what this is all about, or are we looking for more?

Additionally, there are a number of other things observable in the life of church communities today—a new emphasis on denominational identity; bioethical and socioethical challenges around issues like the death penalty, abortion, homosexuality, and the blessing of same-sex unions—and one would have to say that the goal of the ecumenical movement has become less clear. The ecclesial walls today have become more porous, but not necessarily in a positive way. It is not uncommon to hear people speak of "double-belonging." Young adults, often unfamiliar with the protocols resulting from our divisions, frequently ignore them: impromptu eucharistic sharing takes place frequently, and interchurch couples sometimes marry in the partner's church without going through formal procedures in their own to ensure that the marriage will be recognized by both churches.[2]

Has the destination of Christian unity become a blur on the horizon? Let's lift the window shade and picture our destination in both sunlight and shadow. The modern Christian movement called *ecumenical* seeks to recapture the fundamental biblical truth that the church as the people of God and the Body of Christ must exemplify in this world how God gathers people together from the ends of the earth to live as a new humanity. Christian unity is not an isolated end in itself, but must always be understood as unity in and for the world. The key point is that a divided world may see the church and its unity and realize that the church is a stage on the way toward the restoration of the world's own unity.

That vision is contained in the root of the word itself. *Ecumenism* and the adjective *ecumenical* are derived from the Greek word *oikoumene*, referring to the whole inhabited world as one household (*oikos*). Gradually, the term came to refer to the whole church or to the whole faith of the church, as opposed to that which is partial.[3]

The World Council of Churches (WCC) contributed to clarity of purpose in laying out what biblical elements all churches must see as necessary if full reconciliation is to be achieved. These elements include: (1) common confession of the apostolic faith; (2) removal or reinterpretation of past condemnations and mutual recognition of one another as churches; (3) celebrating the same baptism, sharing the Lord's Supper or Eucharist, and sharing a reconciled, ordained ministry; (4) common mission and witness in the world; and (5) common ways of deciding and acting together accountably.[4]

The early history of the WCC is illustrative. From the early twentieth century, the movement's three priorities have been social justice, doctrine, and mission. These three streams eventually flowed into one. The Life and Work Movement, seeking to enable a common Christian response to the victims of war, poverty, oppression, and natural disaster, held its first world conference in Stockholm in 1925; the Faith and Order Movement, desiring the resolution of questions around mutual recognition of members, ministers, sacraments, and governance, met for its first world conference at Lausanne in 1927; and the International Missionary Council, carrying the concern for cooperative mission and evangelism, held its first world conference in Jerusalem in 1928. In 1948, the Life and Work and Faith and Order Movements came together to form the WCC, and in 1961, the International Missionary Council also merged into the WCC.[5]

The Third Assembly of the WCC in New Delhi, India, in 1961, issued what has become a classic definition of the visible unity sought:

> We believe that the unity which is both God's will and his gift to his Church is being made visible as all in each place who are baptized into Jesus Christ and confess him as Lord and Savior are brought by the Holy Spirit into one fully-committed fellowship, holding the one apostolic faith, preaching the one gospel, breaking the one bread, joining in common prayer, and having a corporate life reaching out in witness and service to all and who at the same time are united with the whole Christian fellowship in all places and all ages, in such wise that ministry and members are accepted by all, and that all can act and speak together as occasion requires for the tasks to which God calls his people.[6]

The Second Vatican Council (1962–65) brought the Catholic Church onto the playing field with its Decree on Ecumenism, which recognized the modern ecumenical movement, begun under Protestant initiatives, as the work of God.[7] The decree encouraged Catholics to learn about other traditions of Christian faith and to benefit from the various gifts offered by these traditions in the Body of Christ. The Council also provided the momentum for the creation of national and international dialogues with these other traditions toward a restoration of full, visible unity among them.

In 1991, the Assembly of the World Council of Churches in Canberra, Australia, described the marks of what it called "full communion":

> The common confession of the apostolic faith; a common sacramental life entered by the one baptism and celebrated together in one eucharistic fellowship; a common life in which members and ministries are mutually recognized; and a common mission witnessing to the gospel of God's grace to all people and serving the whole of creation.[8]

The Canberra statement went on to say that the goal of full communion would be realized when all the churches were able to "recognize in one another the holy, catholic and apostolic church in its fullness." It further specified that full communion would be expressed on the local and universal levels of the church through councils and synods.[9]

KOINONIA

Toward the close of the last millennium, the highest decision-making body in the community of apostolic life to which I belong, the Paulist Fathers, expressed the desire to open an office that would give more visible expression to the community's commitment to the work for Christian unity. Shortly thereafter, I was invited to open and develop the work of a Paulist North American Office for Ecumenical and Interfaith Relations. In the first year, I began a quarterly journal/newsletter and gave it the Greek name of *Koinonia*. Since we have learned other foreign words—*mañana*, *quid pro quo*, *sayonara, carpe diem, ciao, status quo, adiós*—and made them part of our normal discourse, why not make *koinonia* part of our language with one another in our life together as Christians?

Depending on its context, the word is variously translated in the New Testament as "communion," "participation," "sharing," and "partnership." The noun *koinonia* (in Latin, *communio*) derives from a verb meaning "to have something in common, to act together." It appears in passages recounting the sharing of the Lord's Supper (see 1 Cor 10:16–17), the reconciliation of Paul with Peter, James, and John (see Gal 2:7–10), the collection for the poor (see Rom 15:26), and the experience and witness of the Church (see Acts 2:42–45). It is both gift and task, involving accountability to one another and to Christ.

The word *koinonia* is used in the New Testament to speak of our union with God in Jesus Christ through the Holy Spirit. It is a gift of the Spirit, a grace which enables us to believe in Jesus Christ and thus have real community with one another.

In other words, the church is a community of all those reconciled with God and with each other because it is a community of those who believe in Jesus Christ and are justified through God's grace.

Christians often describe the mystery of unity among the persons of the Trinity as communion. It is this communion that should find visible reflection in our Christian life in the community of the church—a common life in which all the branches form part of the one vine.

Christ invites us into an ever deeper communion, to that fullness where division and barriers in our human lives are overcome, and differences and diversity no longer lead to discord, but are found to reflect the richness and fullness of the life of God. The more *koinonia* we have, the more we long for it to be complete. Its core meaning in New Testament usage is a shared experience of something beneficial that is greater than ourselves, both individually and as separated communities.[10]

What is that "something beneficial"? At the heart of *koinonia* is the eternal mystery of the communion that is the very life of God. We participate in this communion in and through the Body of Christ and the Holy Spirit given at Pentecost. Consequently, if the life of the Christian and of the church is life originating in the Spirit and life of Christ, then the central motif of our spirituality will be communion. Our lives and that of the church must therefore be shaped by a spirituality of communion. *Koinonia* is the essence of what it means to be the church.[11]

The church is a communion of life exuding from the *koinonia* of the Trinity. As the giver of the life of faith, the Holy Spirit is both agent of unity and actualizer of diversity in the church. Unity: the church is a communion of believers in Jesus Christ, and the Holy Spirit is the church's principle of unity. Diversity: the Spirit sustains diversity as gift within a fundamental oneness. Efforts to understand difference, and to discern between differences that are divisive and differences that are not church-dividing, are manifestations of the Spirit at work with us as a partner in our efforts to overcome division. The Holy Spirit works unceasingly to restore and renew Christian communion broken by differences that lead to division. Not only is the Spirit of God a key partner in dialogue, but the Spirit *is* the dialogue among Christians because the Spirit is the dialogue between Father and Son. It is therefore not the church that possesses the Spirit, but the Spirit who claims the church and is its sustainer and animator. It is the Spirit within us and among us who is leading us toward God's future of full and visible unity for the church as we remember the past and live in the present of our salvation history.[12]

In our pilgrimage toward the kingdom of God, our communion with one another as Christians will always be fragile and subject to injury. Furthermore, it will always be a communion tending toward the fullness that will only be realized in the eternal kingdom. In our deeply divided world, it is hard to imagine what full communion might look like. Yet, we are all assured that Jesus Christ has broken down the dividing walls and brought all of us into God's household. Christians are called to give this unity visible expression in the human family. The dream of full communion is expressed in exuberant images of peace among nations, abundant harvest, and the enjoyment of family and friends who come together.

The word *koinonia* appears twenty-two times in the New Testament. The context for its usage is a reflection on how the church shares in and is shaped by salvation, and shares that salvation with others. For example, we are called by God into the fellowship of his Son (see 1 Cor 1:9). We share in the gospel (see Phil 1:5). We share in Christ's body and blood in the bread we break and the cup we share at the eucharistic table (see 1 Cor 10:16).

Koinonia/communio is also the key concept for all bilateral and multilateral dialogues—from those with the Orthodox, Anglicans, Lutherans, and Reformed to those with Evangelicals and Pentecostals. They all converge in that they define the visible unity of Christians as *koinonia* or *communio*-unity, and they agree in understanding it by analogy with the original trinitarian model, that is to say, not as uniformity but as unity in diversity and diversity in unity.[13]

In one of its Agreed Statements, the U.S. Lutheran–Roman Catholic Dialogue provided a basic exposition of the unity we share in its book, *The Church as Koinonia of Salvation: Its Structure and Ministries*.[14] *Koinonia* characterizes not only the way we receive salvation but also the way it is offered to others through the church, whether through sharing the gospel with seekers or sharing our material resources with the poor and the needy. So communion with God through Jesus Christ in the Holy Spirit has not only a theological but a communal and social dimension as well, especially communion with the suffering; it has both a vertical and a horizontal dimension.

Salvation has called forth a type of community, the church, which we hope is coherent with the grace and calling received. It is both a vertical and a horizontal fellowship with God and fellow believers (see John 1:2–7), a life lived with love, in faith and trust, and marked by hope. It relates to the world not merely as one social institution among others, but as a sign of God's will that all share in salvation. It should not then be difficult to see how divisions within the community of the church blunt the impact of our witness to salvation.

This understanding of the church, called a "communion ecclesiology" by theologians, was recognized by the 1985 International Synod of Bishops in the Roman Catholic Church as "the central and fundamental idea" of the documents of the Second Vatican Council. The documents of the Second Vatican Council present a variety of images and concepts that surface in the description of the nature of the church: the church as the people of God, as Body of Christ, as Temple of the Holy Spirit, as sacrament (sign and instrument of unity). A detailed analysis, however, reveals that these images and concepts are ultimately based on and interpreted through the understanding of the church as *koinonia/communio*.[15]

Communion—both mystical and practical—is what holds the church together. It is already given, but there's still more to receive, so we may speak of the communion we have and the communion we seek. Communion with God the Holy Trinity and with one another in the Body of Christ is a mystical reality, unfathomable in its depth of meaning and infinitely precious. As such, it carries an imperative and involves obligations to deepen our communion with one another.

THE CHURCH:
TOWARD A COMMON VISION

As we have noted, this understanding of the core of the church's unity is reflected in ecumenical documents as well. In 2012, the World Council of Churches' Faith and Order Commission presented to the WCC's Central Committee the fruit of two decades of dialogue on what has long been identified as the most elemental theological objective in the quest for Christian unity: a global and ecumenical vision of the nature, purpose, and mission of the church.

For nineteen years (1993–2012), the delegated representatives of the Orthodox, Protestant, Anglican, Evangelical, Pentecostal, and Roman Catholic Churches have met in various fora of dialogue and countless drafting meetings to arrive at a common—or convergence—statement on ecclesiology titled *The Church: Towards a Common Vision*. At the 2013 WCC General Assembly in Bhusan, South Korea, all the member churches were requested to give the statement careful study and provide their official response by the end of 2015.[16] The commission believes that its reflection has reached such a level of maturity that this convergence text has the same status and character as its all-time "best-seller," the 1982 document, "Baptism, Eucharist, and Ministry,"[17] which has been a basis for many "mutual recognition" agreements among churches and remains an important resource today. *The Church* acknowledges that the "biblical notion of *koinonia* has become central in the ecumenical quest for a common understanding of the life and unity of the Church."[18]

The first objective of *The Church: Towards a Common Vision* is renewal: "The churches reading this document may find themselves challenged to live more fully the ecclesial life; others may find in it aspects of ecclesial life and understanding which have been neglected or forgotten; others may find themselves strengthened and affirmed." The second objective is theological agreement on the Church.[19]

The convergence reached in *The Church* represents an extraordinary ecumenical achievement. While it does not represent full consent on all the issues considered, it clearly expresses how far Christian communities have come in their common understanding of the church. It shows both the progress that has been made and the work that still needs to be done. As such, it is a significant step toward the WCC's aim of serving the churches as "they call one another to visible unity in one faith and one eucharistic fellowship, expressed in worship and common life in Christ, through witness and service to the world, and to advance to that unity in order that the world may believe."[20]

Such statements and the work that has gone into them clearly indicate that within the ecumenical movement, there is a strong commitment to the goal of visible unity. As well, there has been a growing awareness that such unity calls for structural expressions that make it concretely visible. Today, however, in our pluralistic culture, to say as much is to swim against the current, for there seems to be an increasing inclination to exchange the goal of visible unity for a basically friendly and largely invisible coexistence in which the different churches mutually accept one another as they are.

The president of the Pontifical Council for Christian Unity, Cardinal Kurt Koch, gave a bracing assessment of the present pattern in his talk at the Catholic University of America:

> On the part of the churches and ecclesial communities of the Reformation above all, the originally envisaged goal of visible unity in the shared faith, in the sacraments and in ecclesial ministry has steadily been abandoned in favor of a postulate of mutual recognition of the various churches as churches, and thus as parts of the one church of Jesus Christ. That such a goal must be considered insufficient

and in contradiction to the theological principles of Catholic and Orthodox ecumenism has been expressed in clear words by Pope Benedict XVI: "The search for the re-establishment of unity among divided Christians cannot therefore be reduced to recognition of the reciprocal differences and the achievement of a peaceful co-existence: what we yearn for is that unity for which Christ himself prayed and which by its nature is expressed in the communion of faith, of the sacraments, of the ministry. The journey towards this unity must be perceived as a moral imperative, the answer to a precise call of the Lord."[21]

In what does the full communion to which Pope Benedict refers consist? In the Second Vatican Council's Dogmatic Constitution on the Church (*Lumen Gentium*, 1964), four bonds are cited: professed faith, sacraments, ecclesiastical government, and fellowship (no. 15). In this model of "organic union," the church is seen as a complex reality: it is both a spiritual community and a sacramental, hierarchical society. As such, for Catholics, full communion involves participating in the life of the church sacramentally and juridically as well as spiritually. This means that full ecclesial communion involves a network of different kinds of bonds linking people to the church and to one another.

Thus, Roman Catholics are in "theological communion" with other Christians in grace, faith, and sacramental life (baptism). However, our communion is imperfect inasmuch as our lives are not characterized by the fellowship that binds Catholics together in the life of the church as a community and is expressed in eucharistic sharing. Nor are they characterized by the "juridical communion" resulting from the common bonds of ecclesiastical government (parish pastor, diocesan bishop, pope) involving mutual recognition of rights and duties between church members. The Catholic Church's vision of full visible unity is one in which Christians are held together by the bonds of faith, sacramental life, pastoral governance, and mission.

Over the past forty years, a number of denominational churches have opted for another model of church unity, that of "reconciled diversity," in which the churches preserve their historic identities and methods of decision making while sharing in sacraments, ministry, and mission.

This model of unity indicates that the way forward is not one church absorbing another or becoming exactly like another. It allows some space where the distinctive identity of each of the historic traditions of Christian faith is preserved. It recognizes the fact that churches are the product of a long history and context that does make each one unique in some respects. Any expression of unity must honor that uniqueness in some way. To work for unity means forging communion in the face of difference.[22]

UNITY IN DIVERSITY

The overarching characteristic of trinitarian life is unity in diversity. As the *Directory for the Application of Principles and Norms on Ecumenism* observes:

> The unity of the Church is realized in the midst of a rich diversity. This diversity is a dimension of its catholicity. At times the very richness of this diversity can engender tensions within the communion. Yet, despite such tensions, the Spirit continues to work in the Church, calling Christians in their diversity to ever deeper unity.
>
> This unity by no means requires the sacrifice of the rich diversity of spirituality, discipline, liturgical rites and elaboration of revealed truth that has grown up among Christians in the measure that this diversity remains faithful to the apostolic tradition.[23]

The Church: Towards a Common Vision provides clear reassurance that the unity of which it speaks is not uniformity but a communion in unity and diversity. Plurality, diversity, is attested to in the writings of the founders of our faith. The one Lord Jesus Christ inspired four Gospels, four different proclamations with variances among them.

> Legitimate diversity in the life of communion is a gift from the Lord. The Holy Spirit bestows a variety of

complementary gifts on the faithful for the common good (1 Cor 12:4–7). The disciples are called to be fully united (Acts 2:44–47; 4:32–37), while respectful of and enriched by their diversities (1 Cor 12:14–26). Cultural and historical factors contribute to the rich diversity within the Church. The Gospel needs to be proclaimed in languages, symbols and images that are relevant to particular times and contexts so as to be lived authentically in each time and place. Legitimate diversity is compromised whenever Christians consider their own cultural expression of the Gospel as the only authentic ones, to be imposed upon Christians of other cultures.

At the same time, unity must not be surrendered. Through shared faith in Christ, expressed in the proclamation of the Word, the celebration of the sacraments, and lives of service and witness, each local church is in communion with the local churches of all places and all times. A pastoral ministry for service of unity and the upholding of diversity is one of the important means given to the Church in aiding those with different gifts and perspectives to remain mutually accountable to each other.[24]

From the beginning, Jesus Christ makes room for diversity, which we can understand as enrichment (Jewish Christians, ethnic Christians), and belief in Christ is enmeshed within a diverse range of communities. This diversity is not negated but absorbed in the New Testament scriptures, in the liturgies, and in the life of the churches. The Catholic Church itself is a communion of diverse churches, including the Latin (Western) Catholic Church as well as twenty-two Eastern Catholic Churches rooted in the Byzantine, Alexandrian, Antiochian, Armenian, and Chaldean traditions. Each one has its own liturgical, spiritual, theological, and canonical traditions.

On the other hand, diversity is not unconditional. The most important condition for diversity is that it must not destroy unity. In the words of Saint Maximus the Confessor, "difference" is positive, but must never become "division."[25]

In 2010, the National Council of Churches in the USA met in New Orleans, Louisiana, in a centennial gathering to celebrate the beginning of the ecumenical movement in 1910 in Edinburgh, Scotland. A draft document, "Christian Understanding of Unity in an Age of Radical Diversity,"[26] served as a springboard for reflection and discussion, some perspectives from which are shared here.

Unity and diversity must be held in dialectical tension in any faithful understanding of the church. The unity sought is that "of a living organism, with the diversity characteristic of the members of a healthy body."[27] Holding unity and diversity together in tensive balance is a challenging exercise. Unity is only meaningful if it includes those who are not alike, for example, human diversities of race, gender, culture, and theological perspectives on the one faith.

Similarly, diversity without concern for the common good can become fragmented and provincial. Overemphasis on diversity or unity can have destructive consequences. Blaise Pascal said as much in the seventeenth century when he suggested that "diversity without unity leads to confusion, while unity without diversity is tyranny."[28]

The New Testament does not call the church to be diverse. Diversity is an evident, God-given reality. However, diversity can easily become difference that leads to division. "The goal of the ecumenical movement is not to unite those who are diverse—that is the goal of political parties and governments. The goal is to celebrate the wondrous diversity of our God-given oneness as God's people."[29]

The unity which the Apostle Paul urges is a unity *of* diverse members, not a unity imposed *over* diverse members: "For as in one body we have many members, and not all the members have the same function, so we, who are many, are one body in Christ, and individually we are members one of another. We have gifts that differ according to the grace given to us" (Rom 12:4–6).

When the "body of Christ" passages in the New Testament letters such as 1 Corinthians (see 12:12, 27), Ephesians (see 1:22–23; 4:4–6), Romans (see 12:4–5), and Colossians (see 1:17–18, 24) are looked at closely, we see that none of them say simply that the church is *like* the body of Christ. Rather, they make the startling claim that the church *is the Body of Christ.*

> To put it simply, the church is not its own. The church is not self-generated or self-directed. The church is not its own, for the church belongs to another, to Christ, precisely

as Christ's body. The church is not master of its own life, able to determine its own nature or purpose, for the church belongs to Christ alone. Even so, the bond of *church and body of Christ* is not a natural one, as if the church were the continuing form of Christ's earthly presence, or as if the church dwells in Christ's heavenly presence. Rather, as the body of Christ, the church exists as a visible collection of ordinary people that is nothing less than the locus of the real presence of Christ.

To call the church "*the body of Christ*" is to set forth the God-given, Christ-shaped, Spirit-empowered unity of the church. The human body is not a voluntary alliance of independent eyes, ears, hands, feet, hearts and lungs; the parts of the body have no viability apart from their bodily unity. As Christ's body, the church is not merely a humanly diverse collection of self-sufficient communities with the brand name "Christian." Christ is so present in this body that the church is not its own, but Christ's.[30]

The purpose for all the communities that make up the church is building up the Body of Christ. The diversity of gifts is to be exercised for the health and maturity of the whole body. Thus, ecumenism is supposed to make us richer and not poorer. Can any church afford to neglect or refuse a single one of God's gracious gifts that may have been better preserved in another tradition of the faith?

The Holy Spirit does not only tolerate ecclesial diversity but actively generates and sustains such diversity, holding it together within the one Body of the church. As Pope Francis expressed:

It is true that the Holy Spirit brings forth *different charisms* in the Church, which at first glance, may seem to create disorder. Under his guidance, however, they constitute an immense richness, because the Holy Spirit is the Spirit of unity, which is not the same thing as uniformity. Only the Holy Spirit is able to kindle *diversity*, multiplicity and, at the same time, bring about *unity*. When we try to create diversity, but are closed within our own particular and exclusive ways of seeing things, we create division. When we try to create unity through our own human designs, we end up with uniformity and homogenization. If we let ourselves be led by the Spirit, however, richness, variety and diversity will never create conflict, because the Spirit spurs us to experience variety in the communion of the Church.

The diversity of members and charisms is harmonized in the Spirit of Christ, whom the Father sent and whom he continues to send, in order to *achieve unity* among believers. The Holy Spirit brings unity to the Church; unity in faith, unity in love, unity in interior life. The Church and other Churches and ecclesial communities are called to let themselves be guided by the Holy Spirit, and to remain always open, docile, and obedient. It is he who brings harmony to the Church.[31]

At the same time, we must recognize that diversity has its limits. One such limit is our obligation to unity. That *one* body is to lead a life worthy of its calling in *one* faith and *one* hope because there is *one* Spirit, *one* Lord, *one* God and Father of *all*. Seen in this perspective, appropriate ecclesial diversity should not necessarily be regarded as an endorsement of parochial identities, but as something that creates the space required for sharing our diverse gifts with each other within the framework of communion. True and sustainable diversity is always taken up into the service of unity because it is directed toward building community.[32]

The goal of unity is a mutual recognition of the one faith and the one church in our many forms of church life, a recognition that makes possible a common Christian life and mission. So, to use another image, the unity that we are seeking will be like a fleet of ships sailing together under a common flagship. Each ship in the fleet has its own captain and crew, but they are all using the same map and sailing in the same direction on a common mission. And when there is an important decision to be made affecting all concerned, they pull alongside one another and make that decision together.

Similarly, our unity is like a bouquet of flowers made up, not all of one flower or of one scent, but of many different flowers and of many different scents, which give to the bouquet more beauty by virtue of its diversity. And yet, all the flowers are together in the water—the waters of baptism—and held close by the rim of the vase—the "container" of the Tradition that comes to us from the apostles and the early church and finds expression in the Creed.

One of my favorite images of unity in diversity is that of a large, single-story house with many rooms organized around a common dining room. Each room in the house is decorated differently: one with wood paneling, another with wallpaper, another with stucco, another with tiles. The doors to all the rooms are open, and those who live there spend time in the different rooms, although each one has a particular room within which the clothes are hung, friends received, sleep taken, and work done. Whenever they choose, all who live in the house can come together around the common table in the dining room to share food together. While being built on a common, stable foundation, the diversity of style and décor that characterizes the different rooms makes the house more attractive and interesting.

The rooms are the different Christian traditions: Anglican, Baptist, Lutheran, Orthodox, Reform, Roman Catholic, Evangelical, and Pentecostal. The house's foundation is our agreement on Scripture, creeds and councils of the early undivided church, mutual recognition of sacraments and ministries, and engagement in common mission. The unity we seek will enable us to step back and look at that house and say, "I live there with all my brothers and sisters. And the *whole house*—not just my room in it—is mine!"

In short, we have a positive commitment to diversity grounded in a fundamental unity, affirmed and celebrated as a rainbow gift of the Creator. The Christian scriptures see legitimate variety as a gift of the Holy Spirit, something to be received with gratitude and joy and to be cherished.

Diverse groups and denominations are called to strive side by side with one mind, to live out their unity in faith synergistically. So the task of the churches is to give complementary and therefore unified witness to their faith in the gospel of Christ. We are urged to unity in faith and life, theology and morality, doctrine and ethics, evangelism and justice. This witness should not be obscured by the emphasis that tends to be given to historical and sociological diversity.

As the gospel is brought into different cultures and contexts, it is the effectiveness of mission that is the real source of diversity in the church. Diversity of expressions of the gospel is an instrument of mission—inculturation—and corresponds to the diversity of cultures. However, just as mission creates diversity, it also demands unity, so that the diversity remains grounded in the one gospel. Unity is not opposed to diversity, the opposite of which is uniformity. And by the same token, diversity is not opposed to unity, the opposite of which is division. Therefore, if we set our compass against both division and uniformity, we should find ourselves steering a course toward unity in diversity.[33]

UNITY BY STAGES

We began this chapter with the analogy of the ecumenical movement as a plane journey, and proceeded to look not only back at the last hundred-plus years but forward to our destination as well. The ecumenical goal is a mutual recognition of the one faith and the one church in our many forms of church life, a recognition that would make possible a common Christian life and mission.

What about our present position in the air? Some of the faithful in our congregations are grateful that what was once a hard-to-pronounce word (*ecumenism*) has become a lived reality in their neighborhoods. Others complain that the wonderful and pleasing work of all the dialogue commissions doesn't seem to be finding implementation at local levels. Others are disappointed with the work of ecumenism, because they are impatient for the "thorny questions" between the churches to be tackled and solved.

Certainly, there are still some substantive disagreements among us, so the way forward will be slow and messy. While some success has been achieved in overcoming old denominational differences of faith, today it is mostly significant differences in ethical questions that come to the forefront. In an earlier phase of the ecumenical movement, the slogan was "Faith divides, action unites." Today that adage has been altered and inverted: "Ethics divide, faith unites." And one of the fundamental questions underlying this phenomenon is whether and to what extent it is legitimate for Christian churches to adjust their own ethical standards to the spirit of the times, or whether they must distance themselves from it. Further, given that these ethical questions involve the human image, a related task before us is the development of a common ecumenical anthropology.[34]

Essentially, we are working for unity by stages. If progress is to be made by the dialogues on doctrinal questions, we need a clearer sense of the sort of consensus we are seeking. Total agreement is not a realistic goal, for how many people completely agree on anything? The current methodology that has made breakthroughs on critical questions possible is known as "differentiated consensus." With this method, the consensus sought is agreement on some aspects of a topic (those aspects central to Christian faith, life, and mission), while allowing for diversity or a difference of emphasis on other aspects of the same topic.

Such was the case, for example, with the 1999 Catholic–Lutheran Joint Declaration on Justification by Faith, which the World Methodist Conference signed onto in 2006. Sufficient consensus is sought to make possible that common life, witness, and mission without which the church cannot be one. One must differentiate between what one thinks is sufficient and what one thinks is best, but not essential, and only insist on the sufficient. A reconciled church will inevitably be one in which we all must put up with things we don't much like, but which do not compromise the faith in any essential way.[35]

Unity among Christians is one of those realities that is already there, but not yet fully—and may never be "full" until the end-time because this *koinonia* can only be realized through a deeper mutual participation in the life and love of God through grace. It can only be the result and expression of the communion that Christians have with the Father and the Son through the Holy Spirit and therefore with each other. In the end, it's personal, relational, and spiritual.

That's not to say that church structure has no importance in Christian unity. The spiritual cannot exist without the structural in this created world. The unity we seek is not something ethereal and invisible that is without expression in the enfleshed reality of our earthly lives. The church's existence is patterned on the incarnation of Christ. In other words, divinity is embodied.

The unity of the church is given in Christ; we could not and will not produce it. Our task is to make it visible for the glory of God and the benefit of all humankind. Common ecclesial structures can play a key role in visualizing unity and in serving more efficiently its mission in the world. The church is no mere "idea," but a Body, and like any body, it has and needs structures—for its ordained ministries, communal worship, teaching, and decision making. Such common structures for mission reflect the crucial fact that church unity is not an isolated end in itself, but must always be understood as unity in and for the world. In this way, the church can be an effective and credible sign of unity in a deeply divided world.[36]

That said, we also know that ecclesial structures are provisional and imperfect. Nevertheless, it seems to be God's will that the church on earth should be an embodied (that is, structured) community—one that is ordered to its task of mission and equipped with all the means of carrying it out. And if God wills such structures, God must know that such structures are capable of serving, enhancing, and embodying that personal, relational *koinonia* that is the essence of unity.[37]

THE UNICITY OF THE CHURCH

In its convergence statement, *The Church: Towards a Common Vision*, the Faith and Order Commission's work on the main obstacle —our understanding of the church and of unity—will I hope be taken seriously by the churches and move the ball forward on the field.

For Catholics, other churches and ecclesial communities— Orthodox, Anglican, Lutheran, Reform, Evangelical, Pentecostal— are Christian communions in which the means of grace are available and in which communal worship is offered to God. The process of sharing in the life of Christ takes place within each community of faith and by means of it.

In other words, these churches and ecclesial communities are within the Body of the one church of Christ. This understanding is based on the unicity of the church. Since there is and can be only one church, it follows that there can be "churches" only insofar as in some real way they all participate in the reality of the one church. The universal church has to be understood as a Communion of communions/churches; otherwise, every use of the term *church* in the plural would contradict the oneness of the church that we profess when we say in the Nicene Creed, "I believe in the one, holy, catholic, and apostolic church."

Vatican II recognized that the churches and ecclesial communities admit of greater or lesser degrees of fullness or completeness. The Decree on Ecumenism, released on the same day (November 21, 1964) as the Dogmatic Constitution on the Church, seems to evaluate them on a sliding scale of institutional, quantitative elements that they share with the Catholic Church.

As far as theological communion in faith and sacramental life is concerned, the degree to which Catholics and other Christians can be said to share a common faith will depend on the belief and practices of each particular church. Hence, it is very difficult to make general statements in this regard. Whatever the shortcomings of any of these churches and ecclesial communities might be according to Catholic belief, their nature as "church" and as instruments of salvation for their members is clearly recognized. The 1993 *Directory for the Application of Principles and Norms on Ecumenism* in the Catholic Church stressed the presence and activity of the universal church in the particular churches.[38] Pope John Paul II said in 1995 that "the elements of sanctification and truth" shared by other Christian communities show that "the one Church of Christ is effectively present in them." This is the reason for the communion that persists between the Catholic Church and "the other Churches and Ecclesial Communities" in spite of their divisions.[39] Furthermore, there is no claim that a church having a fuller array of the means of grace will necessarily be a holier Christian community than those perceived to be lacking something. The bottom line is how responsive and devoted we are to what we've been given.

While we have not yet achieved the full visible unity of all Christians, worldwide Christendom has clearly drawn closer together. This is evidenced by the recent emergence of the most inclusive forum for ecumenical dialogue and collaboration yet seen: The Global Christian Forum, which has brought Christians together from around the world in Kenya in 2007 and in Indonesia in 2011.

> The Global Christian Forum is about bringing into conversation with one another Christians and churches from

very different traditions who have had very little contact or never even talked to each other. It is about building bridges where there are none, overcoming prejudices, creating and nurturing new relationships.

We have become convinced that our churches and organizations could benefit greatly from a Forum where they could speak with one another face to face, pray for one another directly, learn from one another, and together gain insights into common problems that could help everyone to respond to them more effectively.[40]

What should be noted here is that despite all the hurdles still before us on the track, Christendom increasingly sees itself as a community of brothers and sisters in Jesus Christ, and understands its duty to bear witness to fraternity and justice and peace among all people in today's world.

PRACTICAL ECUMENISM

The path to the universal passes through the particular. Work for unity among Christians can only start from where we are. We will need humility and modesty about what any step actually accomplishes and the courage to keep the ultimate goal in sight. At the same time, as is the case in any long journey, we will not want to just focus on the destination, but draw joy and fulfillment from the journey itself. There is an increased awareness that we all belong to Christ. As the Decree on Ecumenism confirmed, all those baptized into Christ who believe in God—Father, Son, and Holy Spirit—are our brothers and sisters in Christ. Through baptism, they are "members of Christ's body," "truly incorporated into the crucified and glorified Christ, and reborn to a sharing of the divine life" (nos. 3, 22).

The path to giving full expression to that unity among us as Christians is indeed a long journey. It is a marathon, not a sprint. What has been accomplished in the ecumenical century that lies behind us can provide us with courage and confidence in this new millennium that what the Spirit of God has initiated will continue in ways we cannot predict in our rapidly changing world.[41]

The good news is that the hostility and indifference of the past has largely disappeared, and a process of healing has begun that allows us to welcome the other as a brother or sister in the profound unity born of baptism. The appreciation of what is good and true in the lives of Christians from every community is but one example of the Holy Spirit's work among us.

We are living in an intermediate situation between the "already" and the "not yet fully." The church will always be a pilgrim church on this earth, struggling with tensions and schisms. As a church of sinners, we will never be a perfect church. We will have to distinguish between tensions, which belong to life and are a sign of life, and contradictions, which destroy and make communal life more difficult. We have to apply all that we have achieved to the way we actually live. Historically, the churches did not diverge only through discussion; they became alienated because of the way they *lived*. In this time, we must come closer to one another again in our living. We must become accustomed to one another, praying together, working together, living together, bearing the pain of our incomplete *koinonia/communio* together, and advancing the process of healing and wholeness within the Body of Christ.[42]

Cardinal Walter Kasper, who served as the president of the Pontifical Council for the Promotion of Christian Unity for nearly a decade, wrote in his book *That They All May Be One*:

> This interim stage must have its own ethos: renunciation of all kinds of open or hidden proselytism, awareness that all "inside" decisions also touch our partners, healing the wounds of history (purification of memories). We need a larger reception of the ecumenical dialogues and the agreements already reached. Without danger to our faith or our conscience, we could already do much more together than we usually do: for example, common bible study, exchange of spiritual experiences, gathering of liturgical texts, joint worship services of the Word, better understandings of the common tradition as well as of existing differences, co-operation in theology, mission and cultural and social witness, co-operation in the area of development and preservation of the environment, in the

mass media, etc. It is also particularly important for us to develop a "spirituality of *communio*" in our own church and between the churches.[43]

In this transitional period wherein we have a real though not yet complete communion with one another, we are called to engage in practical ecumenism. Everyone has a contribution to make toward giving our unity as members of the one Body of Christ more concrete and visible expression. It is with that in mind that the next several chapters are devoted to manifesting the concrete, practical things that we church members can do.

3. WHAT *YOU* CAN DO— PARISHES/CONGREGATIONS

The importance of ecumenism at the local level cannot be overestimated. While active leadership by church authorities at higher levels is certainly helpful, in the long run there will be no significant progress toward Christian unity unless the people at the grassroots level of church life get behind it and give it meaningful, visible expression.

The *Directory for the Application of Principles and Norms on Ecumenism* states that "those who are baptized in the name of Christ are, by that very fact, called to commit themselves to the search for unity."[1] It makes reference to the Second Vatican Council's Decree on Ecumenism by lifting up its teaching that "the attainment of union is the concern of the whole Church, faithful and shepherds alike" (no. 5).

The Ecumenical Directory encourages "all the faithful...to make a personal commitment toward promoting increasing communion with other Christians" and emphasizes that "God's call to interior conversion and renewal in the Church, so fundamental to the quest for unity, excludes no one."[2]

In 1998, the Pontifical Council for Christian Unity released a document specifically related to the ecumenical dimension of the formation of those engaged in pastoral work, and reiterated that "the restoration of full visible communion among all Christians is the will of Christ and essential to the life of the Catholic Church. It is the task of all, of lay people as well as ordained."[3]

Pope John Paul II struck a similar note in what was the first encyclical ever entirely devoted to the mission for unity among the followers of Jesus, On Commitment to Ecumenism: "Ecumenism, the movement promoting Christian unity, is not just some sort of 'appendix' which is added to the Church's traditional activity. Rather, ecumenism is an organic part of her life and work, and consequently must pervade all that she is and does" (no. 20).[4]

The Roman Catholic Church may have been late in taking the field in the twentieth-century ecumenical movement, but since its arrival, it has been one of the most committed players on the team of the world's churches that are engaged in moving the ball down the field and closer to the end zone of unity. Its intent and commitments are among the most broad-ranging, detailed, and clear of any Christian denomination.[5] Its focus on spiritual ecumenism as the soul of the whole ecumenical movement is a reminder to all church members that prayer for Christian unity by laity and clergy alike should find regular expression in both our personal and communal times of prayer.

The Decree on Ecumenism exhorted "all the Catholic faithful to recognize the signs of the times and to take an active and intelligent part in the work of ecumenism" (no. 4), praying with and for those of other Christian communions, deepening their own understanding of other Christians, and cooperating with them in addressing social issues (*Ut Unum Sint* 5).

While lay understandings of the work for Christian unity, joint prayer services, common Bible studies, and collaboration in social action have increased over the past fifty years, there are other measures we could be taking to keep moving forward. How many parishes have an ecumenical representative or commission? How often are prayers offered at Sunday worship for Christian unity in general and for the life and witness of other congregations in the neighborhood in particular? How many adult faith formation or catechetical programs integrate the gains being made through the national and international dialogues into their teaching and course material? How many local congregations have a covenant with another or other Christian churches in the neighborhood to express together a shared Christian life to the extent that current circumstances permit?

THE DIALOGUES

Over the past decades, articles and reports on the work of national and international ecumenical dialogue commissions have been posted or published, but how many church members are listening? It is precisely here that unity efforts taking place at higher levels flounder: the fruits of their labors do not successfully make the transition from the national or international dialogue group to the general membership.

People at every level of the church's life—educators, men's and women's congregational groups, parish board members, clergy—need to become familiar with the slow but steady progress being made. There is a hierarchy of truths in Christian teaching, and generally speaking, there is agreement among Christians on those truths considered to be at the top of the list, such as the assertions of faith expressed in the Nicene or Apostles' Creeds. Through the patient and painstaking work of the dialogue commissions, the realm of agreement is becoming broader and deeper. The more aware we become of this agreement, the more we will recognize the real, albeit imperfect, unity with others who have also been baptized into Christ and with whom we share a common membership in his one Body.

In the past fifty years, theologians have done their homework and have reached agreement on many issues that previously divided Christians. Now it is time for local congregations to become more familiar with these consensus statements. Cardinal Walter Kasper's book *Harvesting the Fruits: Aspects of Christian Faith in Ecumenical Dialogue* is but one example of the resources available to parish study groups. In his book, Kasper provides a synopsis of ecumenical consensus, convergences, and differences in the Catholic Church's dialogues with Lutherans, Reformed, Anglicans, and Methodists from 1967 to 2009.[6]

Could we allow our preaching and teaching in adult education programs to be informed and shaped by the results of the interchurch dialogues? To facilitate this, there is a book that looks at the fruits of the dialogues in conjunction with the Catechism: *The Ecumenical Christian Dialogues and the Catechism of the Catholic Church*.[7] That resource is but one indication that there is an increasing accumulation of material to be ingested and digested as the ecumenical truth of our time. Where and when shall we begin? The ecumenical movement is both a grace and a task.

ACTING TOGETHER

At the Third World Conference on Faith and Order of the World Council of Churches held in Lund, Sweden, in 1952, a principle to follow in our ecumenical relations was articulated that has been too little acted upon:

> As we have come to know one another better our eyes have been opened to the depth and pain of our separations and also to our fundamental unity. The measure of unity which it has been given to the Churches to experience together must now find clearer manifestation. A faith in the one Church of Christ which is not implemented by acts of obedience is dead. There are truths about the nature of God and His Church which will remain for ever closed to us unless we act together in obedience to the unity which is already ours. We would, therefore, earnestly request our Churches to consider whether they are doing all they ought to do to manifest the oneness of the people of God. Should not our Churches ask themselves whether they are showing sufficient eagerness to enter into conversation with other Churches, and whether they should not act together in all matters except those in which deep differences of conviction compel them to act separately? Should they not acknowledge the fact that they often allow themselves to be separated from each other by secular forces and influences instead of witnessing together to the sole Lordship of Christ who gathers His people out of all nations, races, and tongues?[8]

"Should we not act together in all matters except those in which deep differences of conviction compel us to act separately?" This question, which has come to be known as the Lund Principle, inverts the typical denominational point of view. It subtly shifts the burden from a council of churches back to its member denominations to judge for themselves the sufficiency of their "eagerness" to "act together in all matters" as far as conscience permits. The Lund Principle urges local churches and their denominational membership to contemplate an entirely different perspective of the interrelationship between them. It calls them to confront the key question of how well they are living out the ecumenical vision of *acting* together.

If we took that principle seriously—"act together in all matters except those in which deep differences of conviction compel us to act separately"—and tried to apply it, there would not be that many things that we would have to do separately. We tend to forget that words like *Episcopalian, Baptist, Lutheran, Presbyterian, Catholic,* and *Orthodox* are *adjectives*. The *noun* is *Christian*. And the noun in a sentence is known as the substantive, because it has more substance than does the adjective, which only has a place in the sentence in virtue of the noun.

Sharing of life and faith is not a question of just occasionally joining hands in a joint project, entered into maybe once a year. Rather, it is a question of renewed relationships and awareness of one another precisely as Christians. Congregational ecumenism means sharing our faith, our tradition, our prayer, our play, our mission in this place where we live together. It involves listening, learning, acting, and communicating.

For many in our congregations, the church's mission for unity is related to something akin to the asparagus on the plate amidst the bread, butter, meat, and potatoes—fine, if you like that sort of thing. But how many relate to it more along the lines of salt and pepper— to be sprinkled over everything on the pastoral plate?

For example, in our prayers of the faithful on Sunday, when we pray for others, how often do we pray by name for the other churches in our city? When we engage in mission to the poor and the homeless, do we share our resources and link hands in collaboration? Must we always have our parish socials or picnics only with members of our own congregation? Would this not also be a way, a time, for us to come together and to begin to know one another? The importance of local ecumenism is seen immediately when one reflects that it is groups of people more than sets of doctrinal propositions, it is communities of belief more than systems of belief, that ultimately need to be reconciled.

HOSPITALITY

Ecumenical hospitality flows from our oneness in Christ. In this movement toward unity, how do we practice hospitality? Are there examples in the life of your congregation where every year you extend a generous and gracious welcome in some way to members of other local churches with whom there is not yet full, visible communion in faith, life, worship, and mission?

When we are in the role of hosting others, whether at a liturgical ceremony, prayer service, or a conference, our hospitality finds expression in our awareness of and attentiveness to others' needs. For example, will our guests be familiar with the rubrics of the service or the behavior expected from participants? A detailed order of service providing the proper cues for standing, sitting, and kneeling will help make the guests feel more secure and at home. Oftentimes, the Lord's Prayer will be prayed. Do we presume that all present are accustomed to pray it in our particular version, or have we printed it in the Order of Service to facilitate easy participation from everyone? And is there seating designated for local pastors who may be attending with their spouses?[9]

If there is to be a prayer service for the Week of Prayer for Christian Unity or an opportunity for the local churches to address their common social and cultural life, the planning should be done together by representatives of the various congregations involved. If the host church takes charge and does all the planning, the others are left feeling like invited guests rather than cosponsors and cohosts. In short, one Christian group does not plan a whole project or ceremony and then, "to make it ecumenical," invites others. Hospitality provides the occasion to exercise Christlike service, not to exert power and control.[10]

Similarly, if we are hosts of the event, we will not want to take for granted the presence of pastors and congregants from other churches. We do not ignore guests that come to our homes but give them a proper welcome. As Diane Kessler notes:

> Ecumenical guests are not a kind of ornament we add to make our ceremony more impressive or to foster an impression of broad-mindedness. The invitees are our brothers and sisters in Christ. Thus, it is not enough, for

example, to *invite* an ecumenical delegation to a liturgical service; it is important to make a *public recognition* that these guests are brothers and sisters, with whom we share many of the riches of Christ's gift to humanity. It can be helpful to stress very simply these common gifts: our baptism in Christ, our love of and obedience to his word, our common appreciation of prayer in Christ. In other words, hospitable recognition of guests is not just publicly acknowledging their presence, but also pointing out their connections with the hosts. Recognizing someone's presence is common courtesy; recognizing his or her connection in Christ is the mark of ecumenical hospitality. Such recognition "teaches" others more eloquently than any document that we are brothers and sisters in the Lord.[11]

We must learn to be both a good host and a good guest. Being a good host means that we are rooted in a particular tradition. The most convicted ecumenically minded Christians are those very involved in their own church life, who know their own tradition well, and who therefore can open the door from the inside to welcome another, and who are very capable of explaining to the others why we do things in this room of our household as we do them, and why it is decorated as it is.

However, we must also learn to be a good guest, which means going to where the other lives, without quitting our own domicile; even going there often enough to get comfortable there and to grow in our appreciation for their distinctive emphases or style and come to see it as truly a gift from their treasure chest to the larger Christian community.

POSSIBILITIES FOR PASTORS

Intercongregational events tend to happen more frequently in parishes and congregations where a pastor or associate pastor has energy and conviction for the church's gospel mission in giving more visible expression to our unity with one another as disciples of Christ. Although, even when such heartfelt passion is present, it's not a cakewalk. In many denominations, congregational membership is on the decline, as is the energy level of an aging clergy. Parish staffs may have shrunk, leaving more on the desk of the pastor. New moral issues have surfaced in the culture wars that represent fresh obstacles to our unity with one another that can have a demotivating effect on our readiness to prioritize time for the get-togethers. The role of pastoral leaders, however, remains an important one, and there is little that is likely to happen ecumenically in parishes where the leadership does not lead or shows little active interest in reaching out to neighboring congregations and their pastors.

Fr. Joe Scott, CSP, an associate pastor at his parish in west Los Angeles, California, shares some of the rewards and challenges of his ecumenical journey with neighborhood pastors.

> When I became a member of the parish staff at St. Paul the Apostle in February of 2007, I realized that we didn't have a relationship with the other Christian pastors in our Westwood neighborhood. There was a vague memory of some encounters in the distant past, but no one on the parish staff seemed to know even the names of the local ministers. In my daily walks, I had come across several churches along Wilshire Boulevard and the area of Westwood Village. I took down their names and then looked up their pastors and phone numbers either in the phone book or online. I knew I wanted to meet our Christian neighbors and wasn't sure how to begin, so decided to simply drop by and introduce myself.
>
> In whatever spare time I had, I visited the pastors of the nearest Lutheran, Presbyterian, Methodist, and Episcopalian churches. I introduced myself as a priest recently assigned to St. Paul's, and desirous of meeting my neighbors. I'm not sure whether it would have been better to phone ahead, or introduce myself by letter, but even though my visits were undoubtedly an interruption in someone's busy schedule, I received a positive reception each and every time.
>
> I enjoyed these initial contacts with my Christian neighbors, but didn't do anything about it for quite a while. In my first year, I was busy learning my pastoral

responsibilities closer to home. In the summer of 2008, I began talking with another member of our parish staff, Pastoral Associate Claire Henning, about the possibility of St. Paul's hosting a gathering of the pastors I had met, along with any others we could find in our area. Claire liked the idea as well.

We went back to the web sites and collected a list of the addresses of the pastors of Village Lutheran Church, University Bible Church, St. Alban's Episcopal Church, Westwood Presbyterian Church, the Westwood Hills Christian Church, the Westwood Hills Congregational Church, the Lutheran Church of the Master, and the Westwood United Methodist Church. We invited the pastors (and associate pastors) to a breakfast at St. Paul's. We also invited Fr. Alexei Smith, the Director of Ecumenical and Interreligious Affairs for the Catholic Archdiocese of Los Angeles, to attend the meeting.

Our agenda was quite simple. We wanted to get to know the other pastors by name and face. We asked Fr. Alexei to share some ways in which local churches could work together. Every participant shared a bit of their own story and the story of their congregation.

My biggest impression of the meeting was that we all genuinely wanted to get to know each other and were pleased to spend this time together. We decided to meet again a month later, and have continued to meet monthly in the years that have transpired since that initial meeting.

At first, our meetings took place in our various church offices. We took turns hosting the meeting place along with a lunch of salad and sandwiches. In the beginning we gave one another tours of our respective church buildings, schools and ministry centers. In recent months, we've begun meeting at a local pizza parlor, which is convenient to all and offers a back room relatively free of noise.

Since the initial meeting, three of the pastors have moved out of the area and others have taken their place. The director of the Westwood Village Christian Science reading room heard about our group and asked if she could attend our meetings. We agreed and she became an enthusiastic member of the monthly sessions until she moved out of the area. We also benefited from the regular participation of a former pastor who was directing a social service agency in the neighborhood until his retirement. A St. Paul's parishioner about to be ordained to the permanent diaconate also heard about the group and has become a regular member.

One of our ongoing discussions has involved what kind of a group we want to be. Some members have urged that we participate in a common project, such as a unified response to the needs of homeless persons in our neighborhood. Other members have felt they most benefited from our group (which we eventually named the Westwood Christian Churches Association) as a more agenda-free fellowship in which we provide support to one another and the freshness of different perspectives on ministering in the twenty-first century in west Los Angeles. At the present time, the more agenda-free mood prevails, but this is a discussion that ebbs and flows.

What remains constant in our meetings is that we typically begin with a short prayer/reflection experience led by different members, and then talk over lunch about the joys, concerns, and frustrations we face in ministering in each of our churches. We talk about projects we're beginning that excite us, and sometimes we visit to show support for one of our members with a particular new project.

In addition to our monthly meetings, we gathered at the end of one summer for a Labor Day cookout hosted by John Woodall, the pastor of Westwood United Church, and his family. At the end of another summer, Claire Henning made her home available for a "day of retreat" which everyone seemed to enjoy. One of our members suggested a local facilitator and we enjoyed a mixture of prayer, sharing and quiet time together in Claire's peaceful back yard.

Since our first meeting in October of 2008, we have organized and participated in formal prayer services during the Week of Prayer for Christian Unity in January, with the member churches taking turns in hosting it, and a preacher from a church other than the host-church to break open the Word of God for us.

In January, 2012, the Westwood Christian Churches Association hosted the city-wide Week of Prayer for Christian Unity Service at St. Paul the Apostle Church, at the invitation of the Southern California Ecumenical Council.

Advent offers opportunities as well. One year, St. Paul the Apostle Church invited our local pastors to proclaim the Scripture for our annual Advent festival of reading and carols. In turn, I accepted an invitation to read a Scripture at St. Alban's festival of readings and carols. The following year, the pastors decided to work together on a booklet of short reflections we composed on the themes of Advent and Christmas. We made copies of "Christmas in Westwood" available to all our congregations.

I have also preached at the Reformation Sunday service at the Lutheran Church of the Master, at the invitation of its pastor. All of these opportunities evolved directly out of the friendships that have been forged among us through our monthly gatherings.

What I can say about our association is that I still look forward to and enjoy our monthly meetings. I find the group a source of fun, wisdom, and fresh perspectives with which to examine my own ministry.

We have discovered that we face common concerns, such as the difficulty of maintaining and nourishing young adult membership, confronting the secularity of twenty-first-century life in Southern California, and thinking "outside" established church structures to find ways of reaching and serving the unchurched in our neighborhood.

One of the roadblocks to moving further along the ecumenical path is the demand that each of our institutional responsibilities places upon us. Our Westwood colleagues share with us the reluctance to add yet one more program or activity to our busy schedules. We have come to see our association of pastors as an inter-congregation support group for ourselves, providing a respite from the many demands facing us on the home front. But those demands continue to make it challenging for us to contemplate any shared endeavor that would involve a significant investment of time and energy.

Another road block on my part is a resistance to *thinking* ecumenically. I haven't yet developed the habit of discovering every St. Paul's parish event—for example Bible study, choir concerts, international pot-luck dinners—as an opportunity to invite members of the other Christian churches in our area to share what we have to offer. Nor do I regularly remember to let our parishioners know via our bulletin and web site about events of possible interests taking place in the other churches in our area. I tend to "think ecumenically" once a month, or for special and rare occasions such as the "Week of Prayer for Christian Unity," rather than as a daily way of viewing my world.

Another challenging factor may be the interest on my part and the part of others in interfaith relationships. The opportunity to get to know members of the local Jewish, Muslim, Buddhist, Hindu, and Sikh communities—which is quite possible in the city of Los Angeles—is relatively new and different and takes some of the energy that might otherwise go to cultivate and deepen relationships with other Christians.

While we pastors have gotten to know and relate to one another in very positive ways over the past several years, the next step for us is to find ways to involve and encourage the members of our congregations to know one another as people, colleagues, and friends. The number of Christians from each of our congregations who have participated in our prayer services for the Week of Prayer for Christian Unity have been a small percentage of the total membership, but those present have always seemed quite interested and excited by the opportunity to meet their neighbors not only during the service but during the coffee and cookie receptions afterward.

There is something to build on here—which might include increasing our hospitality in inviting our Christian neighbors to events which already occur (such as our Christmas festival of carols) as well as finding new ways to work together on a common event, or to create partnerships for meeting a common need. Such strategies could enhance our sense of being truly in relationship with one another as a larger Christian family.

Fr. Joe's account is one that many of those in positions of pastoral leadership will be able to relate to in one respect or another as they look back over their years of experience. As he reflected, "the next step for us is to find ways to involve and encourage the members of our congregations to know one another as people, colleagues, and friends." What form might that take?

PARISH ECUMENICAL REPRESENTATIVES

One approach is to identify someone in the parish who has some fire in the heart for more visible and tangible expressions of unity with other fellow Christians—someone who has the interest and would be ready to give some time and energy to serving as a parish ecumenical representative (PER); someone who could engage others from the parish to contribute ideas and contacts toward deepening relationships with other area churches; someone who could exercise leadership in shaping a few events each year with fellow Christians in the neighborhood or local area.[12]

In short, a PER would be a parishioner designated by the pastor and who has a special role in communicating and coordinating local ecumenical activity.

The desire and the effort to have a PER appointed in each parish receives support from the 1993 Vatican *Directory for the Application of Principles and Norms on Ecumenism*, which states,

The parish, as an ecclesial unity gathered around the Eucharist, should be and proclaim itself to be, the place of authentic ecumenical witness. Thus a great task for the parish is to educate its members in the ecumenical spirit.

This calls for a pastoral program which involves someone charged with promoting and planning ecumenical activity, working in close harmony with the parish priest. This will help in the various forms of collaboration with the corresponding parishes of other Christians.[13]

Mutual support and spiritual nurture are the vital ingredients enabling people to pursue the vision of Christian unity with faithfulness, persistence, and resiliency.

Some of the things the PER might consider making part of his or her responsibilities might include: private and public prayer for the unity of Christians, since prayer is regarded as the "soul of the whole ecumenical movement" (Decree on Ecumenism 8); regular reading that will deepen understanding and appreciation of the ecumenical movement; and taking advantage of opportunities to participate in ecumenically sponsored forums, conferences, and other activities.

Practically speaking, the functions of the PER might look something like this:

> To assist and support the pastor in making the parish a place of authentic ecumenical and interfaith witness
>
> To foster a deeper ecumenical and interfaith awareness among parishioners by inviting parish organizations to look at the ecumenical/interfaith dimension of their program or activity
>
> To encourage and facilitate parish participation in local ecumenical and interfaith activities
>
> To represent the parish, whenever appropriate according to local custom, on neighborhood ecumenical and interfaith organizations or ministries
>
> To serve as a liaison between the parish/Vicariate coordinators/Diocesan Office of Ecumenism

The PER is obviously not intended to carry the ecumenical mission for the whole parish, but rather to be a resource person for the parish, identifying ways in which the parish can be a positive ecumenical and interreligious witness.

If the bishop of the diocese were to ask that each pastor name such a representative, each pastor could then submit the name of the parishioner appointed to this position to the appropriate local, diocesan, or national agencies concerned. The PER will then serve as the contact for the parish. While others may assist the PER in the parish (e.g., an Ecumenical Awareness Committee), the PER works directly with the pastor and is ultimately responsible to him concerning such involvement.

Since the role of the PER is to facilitate the promotion of ecumenical relations and collaboration, the person considered should have organizational skills and an interest in this important work. Nothing can take the place of personal contacts. Meeting and sharing with fellow Christians are primary means of gradually developing practical collaboration in activities and projects that give public witness to how all that we hold together as Christians is broader and deeper than anything that still divides us.

GRASSROOTS ECUMENISM

While attitudes are being developed and education offered within the congregational setting, local opportunities for the translation of ideas into action must also be provided. Initial ecumenical activities and cooperation should be modestly ambitious. Often, too ambitious projects are proposed and never get off the ground. More modest endeavors that can be realized and will be ongoing are far better. They are successful because they demonstrate that ecumenism has to do with some very ordinary experiences in the local parish community. Ecumenism and local collaboration should translate into opportunities for the many, not the specialty of the few. Here are some examples of the possibilities[14]:

1) *Social gatherings* to which other Christians may be invited. Clergy and religious leaders ought to be invited as well so others can meet those they perhaps have heard of but never encountered.

2) *Church socials, suppers, fundraisers, and picnics* as an expression of Christian sharing. Invitations to all Christians in the area could be extended. When they are received, they should be accepted.

3) *Carry news* from other local churches in parish bulletins and inform them of your events.

4) *Place Christmas, New Year's, Easter (and the like) greetings in local newspapers* jointly with other churches.

5) *Place holy day greetings* to the Jewish community, Muslim community, and so on, in local newspapers jointly with other churches.

6) *Use the instruments of social media* like Twitter, Facebook, and blogs to share activities of interest in your communities with one another.

7) *Plan a "Tour of Churches"* with commentary offered on each one's devotional particularities, worship space, furnishings, style, and the like.

8) *Organize an ecumenical concert.* Most churches have choirs. By providing interchurch sponsorship and organizing an arrangement and program committee, an ecumenical concert can be staged readily and successfully.

9) *Lay organizations exchange.* Roman Catholic parish organizations have their counterparts in Orthodox, Anglican, Protestant, and Evangelical congregations whose program activities frequently reflect the same concerns. The exchange provides opportunities for these organizations to get to know one another and to develop some cooperative program areas.

10) *Welcoming and visitation committee.* The function of the committee would include:

   a) Welcoming new neighbors—in person or by telephone—and advising them of the location of churches, synagogues, mosques, temples in the area.

   b) Extending congratulations to a family upon the birth of a child and offering condolences on the death of a member of the community.

   c) During times of illness, visiting sick persons in their homes or in hospitals.

   d) Serving the hospitals, orphanages, homes for the aged, prisons.

11) *Interfaith prayer services.* On national holidays or communal responses to events such as natural disasters or

tragedies such as a plane or train crash, people in the local community experience a natural desire to come together in prayer. Such prayer should be developed with sensitivity to the beliefs and traditions of the partners in dialogue and cooperative activity. Such a service might include the scriptures of the respective religious traditions, silent meditation, and a particular focus on issues involved, for example, freedom, thanksgiving, security, grief, and consolation.[15]

12) *Speaker exchange program.* In the search for mutual understanding, partners in interchurch dialogue extend invitations to competent representatives of each other's denominational traditions to address their congregations on a given topic.

13) *Share occasionally in the actual worship* of other Christians, respecting the discipline of one's own church as well as that of the host church in regard to holy communion.

14) *Share educational facilities, tools, and resources* such as an audio/visual library.

15) *Assess your school textbooks with an ecumenical eye* and with a view to a sensitive presentation of the beliefs of other Christians and other faiths. Check these for distortions and/or negative teaching. Are these texts leading your students away from healthy encounters in the ecumenical movement by placing obstacles in their way? No child is born prejudiced against a religious and/or racial group. He or she is taught this. At home and in school, education in prejudice is for the most part informal, absorbed from the family or from social circles. Some is done, perhaps inadvertently, in school through textbooks and other materials.

16) *Saying grace before meals.* Become familiar with the more common versions used by different traditions of faith. Four traditional ones are listed below:

"O Christ, our God, bless the food and drink of thy servants, for thou art holy always, now and ever and unto ages of ages. Amen." (Orthodox)

"Bless, O Lord, this food to our use, and us to thy service, and make us ever mindful of the needs of others, in Jesus' name. Amen." (Protestant)

"Lift up your hands toward the sanctuary and bless the Lord. Blessed art thou, O Lord, our God, King of the universe, who brings forth bread from the earth. Amen." (Jewish)

"Bless us, O Lord, and these, your gifts, which we are about to receive, from your bounty, through Christ our Lord. Amen." (Roman Catholic)

17) *Gather together congregational leaders* in your neighborhood for a retreat or a daylong meeting to discuss joint activities in worship, education, or service.
18) *Sponsor joint studies* on issues in your town or city such as hunger, economic justice, racism, and human rights.
19) *Hold a mission fair* to share ideas from various denominational mission programs and, if possible, invite visiting missionaries to talk about their work.
20) *Offer a joint vacation church school* sponsored by several congregations in your community.
21) *Plan leadership training* in evangelism, stewardship, or advocacy with other congregations.
22) *Initiate service projects* among area churches to respond to needs such as housing, unemployment, transportation for the elderly and disabled, and care for refugee families.
23) *Form community task forces* on problems such as drug abuse, runaways, nursing homes, or child and spousal abuse with other churches and community organizations.
24) *Organize youth ministries*, especially since churches with small numbers of youth can do much more working together than working alone.
25) *Pray for each other!* Pray for the unity of the church.
26) *Form a community-wide committee of clergy and laity* of all ages to evaluate the local ecumenical situation, arrange prayer services, and pave the way toward a year-round program of joint prayer, study, and action.

27) *Express Christian concern* by taking up a collection on the same day in all churches in the neighborhood for a cause that has commanded the attention of the local community.

28) *Attend the prayer rituals of another faith community* as respectful observers.

29) Encourage local church groups to *include Christian unity concerns in annual programs and projects.*

30) *Organize living room dialogues* on issues that divide us.

31) *Cultivate awareness of each other's gifts.* In receiving a new member from another church, ask, "What gifts do you bring along with you to enrich our life in this tradition of Christian faith?"

32) *Extend an invitation to the neighboring churches* to attend baptisms in a communal setting by sending a few representatives over to welcome the new members into the Body of Christ.

33) *Offer a support group for interchurch and interfaith couples in your parish.* Many dioceses report that over half the marriages blessed by the church involve a Catholic and Christian from another denomination or a member of another world religion. These couples have special needs, often feel isolated in their experience, and benefit greatly from having the opportunity to talk with other couples who are dealing with similar challenges. The parish can offer them space in which to meet and, if possible, accompaniment by a deacon or someone in the parish with a background in religious education or counseling.

As we walk together toward the future, let us make no mistake about it: it is easier to accept division than to work at ending division. The tasks before us today are bound to produce frustrations, but those who are committed to the power of the cross to win a victory over the institutional inertia that confronted Jesus should not be surprised that they themselves are also involved in the same battle, albeit on a different front.

The dynamics of institutional loyalties can tend to cast Christian unity efforts as an unpopular minority movement, but the

Lord will faithfully continue to pull us and prod us in the direction of unity. It cannot be any other way. The imperative to be one is at the center of the Christian faith. We who are made in God's image are called to reflect that unity in diversity that characterizes the life of the Trinity.

In the end, it is a question of obedience. We will be ecumenical only when we are holy, and we will be holy only when we are ecumenical. If the ecumenical movement is in crisis, as some think it is, then so is the church at large, for authentic ecumenism means unity for mission through personal, communal, and church renewal. If such renewal is to be real, the prayer and action outreach of local parishes and congregations are where the rubber hits the road. Ecumenism must be local to be real.

4. INTERCHURCH COUPLES AND FAMILIES

The increased frequency of "mixed marriages" or "interchurch marriages"—in some churches involving 40 to 60 percent of those getting married[1]—warrants more attention than it seems to be getting.

Interchurch couples sharing their lived experience with one another in local groups and in regional, national, and international conferences have carefully chosen the words they use to describe themselves. By using the word *interchurch* as opposed to merely *mixed* marriages, they wish to make it clear that they both remain active in their own church, participate in varying degrees in each other's churches, and both take an active role in the religious education of their children.

Regardless, there is no single blueprint for how they will live this out in their day-to-day lives. While no two interchurch couples are exactly alike, they do share certain common ground intentions. They do not try to convert each other. They do not try to seek out a compromise church ("You give up yours and I'll give up mine, and together we'll go to one that's new for both of us"). They share their faith journeys in positive ways so that they can nurture each other and their children.

When did the couples start connecting with one another and talking about these things? Following the Second Vatican Council, the French group, led by Fr. Rene Beaupère, was the earliest to start bringing couples together and meeting. Soon afterward, an Association of Interchurch Couples in England, under the leadership of Canon Martin, Ruth Reardon, and Fr. John Coventry, was formed. Germans and Austrians were also beginning to meet around that time, although still in small groups and not with formal associations. From the early 1970s, there were international contacts between groups in Europe and beyond.

A Catholic priest from Louisville, Kentucky, Fr. George Kilcourse, attended the Association of Interchurch Families international conference in England in 1988, and he went with others from the United States to the next one, which took place in Northern Ireland in 1990. Inspired by what they saw and heard, they formed the American Association, and it was based in Louisville. Two years later, Fr. Kilcourse's book *Double Belonging: Interchurch Families and Christian Unity*[2] responded to a growing need for helpful resource material.

At the time, I was serving as director of the Canadian Centre for Ecumenism, and wherever I had an engagement in another city or province, I started contacting ecumenical commissions or local councils of churches in advance and asking them if they could organize a listening session with interchurch couples during my visit. The first consultations took place in Edmonton, Calgary, Montreal, Halifax, and Toronto in 1990. Others followed in St. John's, Newfoundland; Charlottetown, Prince Edward Island; and Guelph and London, Ontario.

As is always the case when you have the opportunity to really listen and enter into the reality of what another is living, compassion and solidarity flow from it. I saw how delighted these couples were to discover others like themselves with whom they could share. I saw how isolated some of them felt, in spite of the fact that already back then there were more interchurch marriages in most provinces than same-church marriages. I saw how the divisions of our churches lay a heavy burden on their backs and challenged their ability to live an experience of unity in their home and family life, particularly where worship patterns and participation in the sacraments are concerned. I don't think I have ever interacted with a group of church members who were more grateful that somebody expressed interest in what they were living, and I sought ways to be supportive. In 1996, the Canadian Association of Interchurch Families was born.

A few years later, representatives of associations, networks, and groups of interchurch families in various countries decided to come together internationally. Participants at the Second World Gathering of Interchurch Families held in Rome in 2003 released a paper in which they said,

> We believe that, as interchurch families, we have a significant and unique contribution to make to our churches' growth in visible unity. Many people in our churches have told us that we are pioneers. As two baptized Christians who are members of two different, and as yet separated Christian traditions, we have come together in the covenant of marriage to form one Christian family. As we grow into that unity, we begin and continue to share in the life and worship of each other's church communities. We develop a love and understanding not only of one another, but also of the churches that have given each of us our religious and spiritual identity. In this way interchurch families can form connective tissue helping in a small way to bring our churches together in the one Body of Christ.[3]

In their paper, they indicate that interchurch families describe their experience of participating in the life of two ecclesial communions in various ways—as "double belonging," "double insertion," "double character," and "double solidarity"—not as a canonical category of dual membership, but as a lived reality of experience. By "ecclesial communions," they refer to those autonomous, international or national churches that are variously described as denominations, confessions, communions, or churches.[4]

In short, interchurch couples are bridge builders, concerned to work in harmony with the ministers and congregations where they worship. At the same time, they often find themselves in the tension between the "already" of the unity they experience in their home setting and the "not yet" of the continuing separation of the two church communities of which they are members. There can be a clash between what they wish to do and judge to be right for their family life and its unity, and the often conflicting attitudes and rules of their respective two ecclesial communions. There can be a tension, too, between their authority and responsibility for the Christian education of their children, and the authority and leadership of their two churches for the teaching and governance of their respective communities.[5]

It is important that interchurch couples are received in each other's churches with an understanding welcome. When that is the case, their interchurch character and commitment can become a gift and visible sign of hope for their churches on their path to unity. The Ecumenical Directory of the Catholic Church singles them out as potential "builders of unity."[6] Pope John Paul II's memorable phrase, "You live in your marriage the hopes and difficulties of the path to Christian unity,"[7] pronounced during his visit to England in 1982, has since then become a much cherished dictum for interchurch families worldwide. As Pope Benedict XVI observed, interchurch marriages "can lead to the formation of a practical laboratory for unity. For this to happen, there is a need for mutual goodwill, understanding, and maturity of faith in both partners, and also in the communities from which they come."[8]

The couples are looking for ways in which they can contribute positively to their church communities, and for ways in which they can be nurtured by them as they journey toward deeper unity. The remainder of this chapter will take the form of a conversation with a Catholic and Anglican couple, Ray and Fenella Temmerman, who live in Winnipeg, Manitoba. They worship together in both their parishes and are active in a variety of ecumenical activities. Ray operates the interchurchfamilies.org Web site, as well as an international discussion group where couples share the joys and difficulties, hopes and dreams of their path to Christian unity. They were principal coordinators of the tenth International Conference of Interchurch Families, held in Edmonton, Alberta in 2001.

THE ECUMENICAL JOURNEY: A CONVERSATION

Question: You're actively involved in ecumenism. How did that come about?

Ray: In the small town where I grew up, the various churches worked fairly well together. People knew and respected each other because that is where everyone lived. Our Catholic Church, being the largest, was often the place where large funerals of other traditions were held. So ecumenism wasn't new. It wasn't necessarily called that, it was simply lived. Years later, I became involved in the Theological Students Association of New South Wales, Australia, during my time there studying theology and Scripture. Whereas the former experience of ecumenism was practical, the latter focused more on the academic. Both were very good and were the seeds that grew into the ecumenism I live today.

Then Fenella (Anglican) and I (Catholic) met, fell in love, and married. And that has made all the difference. What was an arms-length issue before became a concrete, particular, personal, lived reality with real impact.

After we married, Fenella and I lived in a rural community in southern Manitoba. There we began experiencing the impact of divided churches. Being part of our worshipping communities was important to both of us, but we were finding that our churches couldn't cope with our both wanting to be involved in both churches as a way of supporting each other in our respective faith traditions. Initially, we thought it was *our* problem. It was only later that we realized that this is the problem of the divided church. This realization gave us a new place of freedom. It was in learning to deal with this problem the churches had, that we began to discover more about our own faith.

As we worked consciously at living within both our churches, Fenella kept asking me about things she saw in the Catholic parish where we worshipped together, and I found myself questioning things I saw in the Anglican parish where we also worshipped from time to time. Unfortunately, her questioning felt to me like an attack on my faith and my church, and I tended to respond either in anger or in silence.

Then one day, she said, "Ray, I'm not attacking you. But if I'm going to live the rest of my life with you, I have to understand what makes you tick." That was a moment of grace for me and the beginning of a different conversation.

Fenella: So we reached a more conscious way of exploring each other's values. Instead of telling each other who we were and whom we thought the other was, we began asking each other what values the other held. We also began listening to the words each of us used to describe those values. We quickly learned that at times we were using different words to express the same shared values. At other times, we used the same words to speak of different values. And sometimes we found we used the same words to speak of the same values! We began learning about and receiving the gift the other had to offer and discovering the richness in each other's traditions.

Ray: We began discovering areas in our own churches where change was needed, if ever there was going to be true Christian unity. We didn't know it at the time, but later came to understand this as "Receptive Ecumenism," a phrase coined by Dr. Paul Murray of the Centre for Catholic Studies, Durham University in England.[9] For me, it's an example of how the "sense of the faithful" is often ahead of the formal/canonical expression of the church.

Question: You're involved in a very specific area of ecumenism, that of interchurch families. How did that begin?

Fenella: As our comfort and understanding grew with each other's spiritual journey and with our churches, I wanted to meet with our Catholic priest. This was very normal for me. We invited him over for supper and had time to talk about our situation. I'll never forget his words: "Canonically, this presents difficulties, but we have to approach it pastorally." He welcomed my taking part to whatever level I felt in conscience I could do. That was great and I participated fully, even teaching Catechism classes to the fifth-grade children and receiving the Eucharist.

Unfortunately, he hadn't shared anything of his welcome to me with key people in the parish. Shortly thereafter, he was moved to another parish and replaced by someone who didn't possess similar pastoral understandings. We were back to square one.

Ray: Suddenly the welcome disappeared, replaced with the priest saying to me, "I can't refuse her, but I wish Fenella would come to the table only at Christmas and Easter."

Fenella: We tried to understand our situation. In a rural community, where life is more transparent, we felt very alone. Ray, however, was determined to understand not only what the rules said, but what they meant. I remember thinking that there can't be many women whose husband's bedtime reading material is the Code of Canon Law!

Meanwhile, our path opened up with a real gift from a friend in England. She had subscribed us to the journal produced by the

Association of Interchurch Families there.[10] I can still vividly remember the first copy we received. Ray stood at our kitchen table, opening the mail. One was a brown manila envelope. As he began to read its contents, I saw tears begin to pour down his cheeks. I joined him and together we read stories of people just like us, people who were living a life of faithfulness in two Christian traditions, and the joys and difficulties of the path to Christian unity. We were no longer alone! Nor were we any longer "the problem."

Ray: There were times when we reveled in what we were discovering about each other and each other's Christian tradition, but also about our own faith and our own tradition. At other times, the going was far more difficult, the conversations between us more challenging, as we struggled to make ourselves understood, and to understand. At times, we had to put aside our discussions on this or that issue, not because it wasn't important, but because it was far too important to force a resolution at the moment. We had to give ourselves and each other time, either to grow in the capacity to say more clearly what we meant, or to hear more clearly what the other was saying. This led in turn to a variety of responses, from "Aha!" moments to "Why did we ever have a problem with that issue?" Through it all, we found ourselves growing in faith, individually and together. Do we agree on everything? Of course not! However, we have learned to respect and value the other in our differences, and to trust God to hold all things together in love.

Over the years, we've listened to each other, translated each other's language of faith into our own, and learned to translate our own faith into the other's language. I've not only come to know and love the Anglican Church, which formed Fenella in her very deep and abiding faith, I've also come to discover, through her eyes, amazing depth in my own Catholic Christian Tradition that I would never otherwise have seen. Through this conversation, we became sacraments of God for each other and felt God calling us into richer and deeper understandings of his love as expressed through various Christian traditions.

Question: So what's the situation now?

Fenella: For years, we were actively involved in the Interchurch Families Movement, meeting others and attending conferences in North America and other parts of the world. Ray administers the interchurchfamilies.org Web site, as well as a discussion Listserv. Ray's job instigated a move to the city, where there is greater anonymity, particularly within the Catholic Church. I feel less involved, but the move has opened up opportunities within both our parishes to work toward care of the environment, as well as some pastoral and social justice work engaging with people of a variety of denominations and no denomination at all. It has brought a richness that now I would miss.

More recently, we have become involved in marriage preparation in our Catholic parish. We don't talk about interchurch marriage, but about marriage as lived in an interchurch context. Just being present has, we believe, given couples "permission" to talk about their traditions, and determine to what extent they want to incorporate both within their marriage.

Ray: At present, the situation of interchurch families varies according to the knowledge and pastoral capacity, or even the whims and wishes, of the pastor. I won't take time to go into what ecclesial life is like for an interchurch couple where bishops and clergy are unaware of the opportunities afforded by the 1993 *Directory for the Application of Principles and Norms of Ecumenism* (DAPNE). Suffice to say that it's all too often a situation of two steps forward and one step back.

Fenella: What we see is that, where mixed-marriage couples are encouraged to be faithful to Christ through their own tradition and welcomed to take part in the "other" tradition to the extent they are able, couples tend much more to remain involved and enthusiastic about their faith. They become truly interchurch, seeing both traditions as "pearls of great price" to be shared with each other, with their children, and with their respective churches. As they are nurtured in their faith rather than being excluded and made to feel unwelcome, the stability and strength of their marriage increases.

Ray: This meets the concern of the Catholic Church expressed in Article 144 of the DAPNE, namely, "In all marriages, the primary concern of the Church is to uphold the strength and stability of the indissoluble marital union and the family life that flows from it." This is important enough to bear repeating. The primary concern is not that the children be raised Catholic, though that is expected of any Catholic parent. Rather, it is "to uphold the strength and stability of the indissoluble marital union and the family life that flows from it." Their children, too, tend to grow in faith and love and participate in their churches, as much as do the children of same-church couples.

Such couples offer prophetic gifts and opportunities for their churches to explore unity, to nurture it in their midst, and to grow together into that unity that is at the heart of God. These churches begin to experience the richness of other traditions as a gift to the Body of Christ, and become more apt to take seriously the journey to Christian unity. They benefit, too, from having in their midst people who take seriously their faith, and live it out in their involvement in their parish communities.

In the process, couples and their churches tend more readily to recognize themselves as mutually responsible for the well-being of the Body of Christ in all its forms, from the reality of the domestic church to the global dimension.

Question: From your experience, what are some things churches could do to encourage mixed-marriage couples to explore and deepen their faith?

Ray: Perhaps I'll begin by saying what I think should not be done. Within the Catholic Church, we should never attempt to deal with the discomfort one may feel in having a Christian of another tradition in our midst by inviting them to participate in the Rite of Christian Initiation of Adults (RCIA) program, in hopes that they will then become Catholic and all the parish's concerns will thereby be dealt with.

The RCIA is an excellent program, but it should be a gift to the participant, not a means of resolving a parish's pastoral tensions. The education program that is part of the RCIA could be offered as a way whereby the Christian of another tradition may come to understand the church of which his/her spouse is a member, with the express understanding that there is no expectation the person will become Catholic. In such cases, however, we would strongly encourage the Catholic spouse to participate fully as well, so they can discuss together what they are learning as they proceed. This will not only increase understanding of the particularities of the Catholic Church, but also increase the communication between and mutual appreciation of the spouses and their traditions, regardless of the ultimate choice of denominational affiliation.

Fenella: I'll add to that by saying that we should not look at the Christian of another tradition as one to be "won over" or *converted*, a term wrongly used in the context. And, should a spouse choose to change affiliation to that of his/her spouse, the event should not be celebrated in a triumphal manner. Remember that the personal and church families from which the person comes may be struggling with what they may perceive as a loss, both for themselves and for the person changing traditions. They, in their faith, are entitled to the same respect we want for ourselves.

Ray: The other thing I'd say not to do is to greet the Christian of another tradition with an exclusionary statement that most won't be able to understand, let alone see any way forward. An example of what I mean here can be found in the United States Conference of Catholic Bishops guidelines concerning eucharistic sharing. In agreement with the DAPNE, part of that statement says:

> For Our Fellow Christians: We welcome our fellow Christians to this celebration of the Eucharist as our brothers and sisters. We pray that our common baptism and the action of the Holy Spirit in this Eucharist will draw us closer to one another and begin to dispel the sad divisions which separate us. We pray that these will lessen and finally disappear, in keeping with Christ's prayer for us "that they may all be one" (John 17:21). Because Catholics believe that the celebration of the Eucharist is a sign of the reality of the oneness of faith, life, and worship, members of those churches with whom we are not yet fully united are ordinarily not admitted to Holy Communion. Eucharistic sharing in exceptional circumstances by other Christians requires permission according to the directives of the diocesan bishop and the provisions of canon law (canon 844 § 4).[11]

It's informative, though only in part. It presumes something highly unlikely, namely, that "the directives of the diocesan bishop and the provisions of canon law (canon 844 § 4)" are known by those present. I suspect even the majority of Catholics in any diocese would be unable to accurately explain those directives and provisions. What chance do Christians of other traditions have?

The language asks no questions, invites no dialogue. It calls no one, not even Catholics, to learn anything more about the Eucharist, or why one should or should not receive. It doesn't teach (pedagogy), and it doesn't reach (evangelization). What should be a pathway to dialogue and understanding becomes, in practice, an unscalable wall without windows or doors, more evocative of a country trying to keep people out, than an institution concerned with the salvation of souls through incorporating all within its embrace.

Fenella: In some dioceses, people are told any permission to receive the Eucharist has to be obtained from the diocesan bishop. I find that most Catholics don't get to speak to their bishop. If that's the case with Catholics, how are Christians of other traditions to manage?

Ray: This issue of eucharistic hospitality raises real questions. The scriptures proclaim, and our churches believe and teach, that in marriage, God makes us one. If that's really the case (and we experience and believe that it is), where is that *one coupled person*[12] to take and eat, take and drink? Surely there must be a way to open the doors to legitimate possibilities.

Question: What would you suggest instead?

Ray: Let's clearly separate the issue of juridical/institutional communion between churches from that of making the Eucharist accessible to individuals of other traditions who are, by virtue of baptism, our brothers and sisters in the household of God. The question is complex, given that the churches attach different significance to what it means for us to receive the Eucharist together. For example, for the Orthodox and Catholic and Missouri Synod Lutheran and some Baptist Churches, it's a sign of unity already realized in faith, leadership, and mission.

For many of the mainline Protestant Churches, it's a way for us to grow together toward the unity we seek. Realistically, in our present context, a positive step forward would be to issue more user-friendly guidelines regarding who might receive, with special consideration given for interchurch couples, who share a level of Christian unity not only by baptism but also by marriage.

The Catholic Church's Code of Canon Law, canon 844, article 4, speaks of persons of faith who (1) have a grave need; (2) are unable to have recourse for the sacrament to a minister of their own church or ecclesial community (which may be because the one coupled person that they are is at this liturgy in this place in the communion of marriage); (3) ask for the sacrament of their own initiative; (4) manifest Catholic faith in the sacrament; and (5) are properly disposed.

We suggest that, rather than simply refer to the criteria, or even state the criteria in a dry and concise albeit accurate way, the criteria be presented as a series of questions, the answers to which will help people determine whether they may, in conscience and with a true welcome from the Catholic Church, receive the Eucharist. These questions might take a form similar to the following:

- Do you have a serious and pressing need to receive the Eucharist?
- Are you unable to attend services of a church or ecclesial community of your own tradition?
- Are you asking for the Eucharist of your own free will?
- Do you believe that, in the Eucharist, you are receiving the true body and blood of Christ?
- Have you been reconciled with God and the church for anything you have done that would stand between you and Christ in the Eucharist?

    If you are a visitor from another Christian tradition, and can say a sincere yes to all five questions, then you are welcome to receive. If you are from another tradition and are considering worshipping here, we invite you to meet with the pastor to discuss the way forward.

Such a series of questions allows the person to enter into the decision-making process by inviting true moral discernment of explicitly stated criteria, rather than simply making statements about criteria referred to but never specified. In addition, it opens the way for catechesis, not only for Christians of other traditions, but for Catholics themselves, many of whom are not aware of the teachings of the Catholic Church on the matter of exceptions for eucharistic sharing.

According to a 2010 Pew Forum survey, only 55 percent of Catholics were aware that the teaching of the Catholic Church was that in the Eucharist, the bread and wine become the body and blood of Christ.[13] Such a series of questions would also change the issue of eucharistic hospitality from a seemingly closed door to, at the very least, an invitation to dialogue, and quite possibly a recognition of exceptional circumstances that would make eucharistic hospitality possible.

Even if the answers to the questions result in the same decision that would come from the direct statements that presently exist, the change in process would go a long way toward ending the exile many Christians of other traditions experience in this situation.

Question: The change in process you speak of would likely have to take place at an authority level beyond the local parish. Are there also things that can be done more locally?

Fenella: The biggest thing one can do to enable and encourage interchurch couples to live their faith to the fullest is simply to recognize them as they are and to welcome them as a gift.

Question: How do you suggest that be done?

Ray: There are a couple of suggestions. The simplest way is to recognize interchurch marriages as such in the parish records. It's an ongoing reminder, and it is then quite easy to issue an invitation to such couples to participate in events geared to their situation.

Second, in marriage preparation programs, having an interchurch couple speak about faithfully living their "double belonging,"[14] thereby modeling interchurch life as a possibility, goes a long way toward validating couples in their marriage across denominational lines. It gives them permission to explore possibilities for their own marriage, and to come to their own decisions as to how they can best live lives of faithfulness to God and to each other in the context of different Christian traditions.

Having spoken of and modeled the reality, it can be helpful to provide some basic information and then ask leading questions. Here's an example of what might be said to couples in a marriage preparation program:

> For those who are marrying someone of another faith, or another tradition within the same Christian faith: In the teachings of the Second Vatican Council, the Catholic

Church expresses respect for the church community or world religion from which the non-Catholic partner comes. While the Catholic partner is called on to do all in his/her power to raise the children with a sound Catholic faith formation, the Catholic Church also recognizes that the spouse who is not Catholic may experience a similar call within his/her faith or tradition. It therefore states that the core value guiding decisions about where and how the couple worships, and how they raise the children, is the strength and stability of the family unit.[15] Here are some questions for your reflection:

- What does my faith really mean to me? What does my partner's faith really mean to him/her?
- How will my faith be perceived in my partner's eyes? How do I perceive my partner's faith?
- In our marriage, will my partner's or my faith be an obstacle between us? How can we make it a strength?
- When we talk about faith, can we easily understand each other? Do we speak the same language? Do we sometimes use the same words to mean different things? Different words to mean the same things? Do we need to get beyond the words to the values each of us holds?
- Is my faith a "pearl of great price" to me? Is my partner's faith a "pearl of great price" to him/her?
- How can I share my "pearl of great price" with my partner, our children, and our extended families in marriage? How can I help my partner share his/her "pearl of great price" with me, our children, and our extended families?
- If our families of origin (whether blood family or church family) put pressure on us to live our faith life in this or that manner, how will we make our own faith choices in life for the health, strength, and stability of our marriage and our family before God?
- How will this be lived out in where we choose to worship and in how we raise our children?

Simply being presented with such questions lets the couple know that it's OK to talk about these issues in their life. That "permission" can be an important first step in enabling the couple to begin exploring and developing their faith, and to begin appreciating and celebrating the gift the other brings.

Fenella: Couples should also be encouraged to approach and involve the pastors of both traditions in preparing for marriage. As Fr. John Coventry, SJ, said in an article he wrote for the British Association of Interchurch Families, "This is part of each taking the other seriously as Christians." He goes on to say that neither partner "should make the mistake of having it all his or her own way and taking charge of the religious side of the marriage. That is not love, and it does not make for a Christian marriage, which can only be created by both partners."[16]

Question: You've spoken about marriage preparation. What is needed for couples already married?

Fenella: Married couples need to know they can share their faith traditions openly, growing in faith and love and understanding as they do so, without the fear that their two-church reality will be looked down upon.

Ray: Even today, the perceived risk in being seen as interchurch couples can seem far greater than any perceived benefit. If things go well in meeting the pastors, they may stand to gain. However, if they already know what is possible and their pastors and fellow parishioners are open to their situation, they have little reason to believe things might be better after the meeting than before. If, on the other hand, things don't go well, they stand to lose whatever safety, security, and stability they have already achieved in the particular way they have chosen to live their mixed marriage. Generally, then, it's better to start small and quietly.

The simplest way to start the process is to personally invite three or four interchurch or potentially interchurch couples to gather together to talk about their marriages. Bear in mind that, despite its prevalence, the interchurch reality is still not often talked about. I'd go so far as to say interchurch couples are, in many places, in a situation somewhat similar to people in the gay and lesbian community twenty-five years ago. They have achieved a certain level of stability in living their marriage reality very quietly. They fear that if they make public their reality, that stability will be jeopardized. Neither they nor the church want that! So they remain silent. It's therefore quite possible that only the parish priest will be aware of who is or is not in such a marriage—and even he may not know many, thinking instead that only one of the spouses is practicing their faith.

Fenella: The aim in such a gathering of couples is not to resolve issues. Instead, it's a time when couples can talk in relative privacy, and therefore more openly, getting to know each other as interchurch couples and learning from each other.

Question: What might they be encouraged to talk about?

Fenella: In the introductory phase, invite them to share a little about how they met. Most couples are comfortable telling that story, and besides, everyone loves a good romance!

Once people know each other a little as interchurch couples, and have had time to absorb something of each other's background, you might ask them whether they talked in their courtship about how they would live their faith as a married couple. Bear in mind that couples may be carrying some guilt, feeling they have fallen short of what they perceive to be expected of them and/or of what they planned to do as regards living out their faith in the context of their marriage. At this point, it's good to stress that what couples talked about, and any plans they made at the time, may or may not be anywhere close to what they actually ended up doing once they were married, especially in those cases where there are children. This is completely normal. Couples may run the gamut, from almost no discussion through to detailed decisions on participation in church worship, baptism, first communion, education, and confirmation of their children. It can be freeing for couples to hear that different people had different approaches and that, whatever ultimately happened, the sky didn't fall.

Ray: One of the most affirming and liberating things you can do in this time is to thank couples for what they are sharing, and to explicitly state that their experience is of value to the church and fellow parishioners. Of course, I'm assuming that you believe this. If you don't, then you're not the person to be hosting such a group!

Question: Are there other areas in life that need talking about?

Ray: There's an often overlooked but very real situation that can be a good subject for discussion with older couples, and that is the area of funerals. Ask two simple questions. The first speaks to the situation of the couple themselves: "When that time finally comes that you pass away, how do you want your spouse to handle your funeral?" The second refers to the life of the parish community: "Regardless of where the funeral is to be celebrated, what can we do to provide support for you during the rites of passage?" This question lets the couple know that their needs are taken so seriously that the parish itself is willing to be helpfully involved. In addition to helping the couple think through the issues, that sense of parish willingness can make the couple feel truly welcome.

Fenella: While many couples don't often talk about this issue until later in life, it's a matter of particular poignancy for interchurch couples. When I die, my spouse will no longer have me to help navigate through the particulars of my tradition. Placing that question squarely in front of people, thereby giving them permission and even encouraging them to talk about it, then going a step beyond to ask what parishes might do to help the remaining spouse, is a real life-giving, liberating, and welcoming action.

Ray: Once we have come this far, the neuralgic issues that are at the forefront of interchurch married life will naturally begin to come to the fore. Among these are the baptism of children, their confirmations, and especially reception of Eucharist. While we encourage the hosts of such a gathering to become familiar with the relevant portions of the DAPNE, for now it is enough to have the issues raised, and begin to be discussed.

Question: Do you have any further comments you would like to share?

Fenella: The late Martin Reardon, speaking to the World Gathering of Interchurch Families in Geneva in 1998, said something that I think is very important for churches to hear. He pointed out that, in marriage, we first commit ourselves to love each other. Then we live under the same roof, share the same resources, make joint decisions about how our family is to live and grow. We learn to compromise on some things, while on other things we learn to let go of precious values because we have come to discover and receive even greater values than those we held. If our churches do not begin to experience a similar reality—committing themselves to love each other, and wherever possible living together under the same roof, sharing resources, learning to compromise for the greater good of the whole, and letting go of our own values in those cases where our relationship has enabled us to discover even greater value—the whole response to Jesus' call that all may be one will reach an impasse. I think interchurch families have something to offer the churches by way of example, in the way we have been called to live our lives.

Ray: Interchurch families are gathering together in various parts of the world. The British Association of Interchurch Families, for example, meets every year at Swanwick. The American Association meets every two years. Other countries such as France, Germany, Austria, and Switzerland have similar patterns. These are very important and valued times for interchurch families. I believe we now need to step out into other areas, into other gatherings of Christian families, to live our interchurch reality as part of the wider events. In some cases, we're doing that, for example, holding panel presentations at theological conferences. I hope the time will come when we see it as quite natural to hold our interchurch family gatherings at major Christian conferences, such as Greenbelt or Spring Harvest in England, or at the same time and place as events such as eucharistic congresses. In so doing, I believe we will be seen as truly part of the wider Christian body, providing a model of service and ecumenism even as we are at the same time invited to grow deeper and stronger within that Christian Body.

Fenella: We actually hosted an interchurch families information booth at Greenbelt in the United Kingdom a few years ago. Being there with twenty thousand other Christians of various backgrounds, traditions, and interests was a wonderful experience, and we had an opportunity to talk with many people. It seemed quite natural. However, a particular situation reminded us that discussing this reality isn't natural for most people. A friend, a competent judge and faithful Christian, offered to give us a break for a couple of hours, something we gladly accepted. On our return, she exclaimed to us, "How do you manage this? I've heard more stories of pain and anguish, frustration and anger, as well as joy that this booth is here, than I can cope with!"

Ray: It gave me real cause for thought. If 20 percent of our congregations were dealing with this or that specific issue, we would be establishing committees to see what could be done to help, setting up workshops, establishing policies, and more. Yet here we have a situation that concerns close to 50 percent of the people in our churches, either as a pastoral concern or as a gift for the ecumenical journey, and it's rarely acknowledged, much less talked about.

It's something for people to think about with an eye to what initiative might be taken in their own local context.

GROWING SPIRITUALLY

Ray and Fenella's witness and sharing provide us with some insights on how couples might grow spiritually in interchurch marriages. The process is not all that different from what would be true for same-church couples: prayer for the help and guidance of the Holy Spirit; active participation in the life of the community of the church, expressed in both prayer and acts of service; and making time for daily prayer.

Such spiritual practices are important for all couples. And spirituality is not something apart from our daily activities but should be something that flows through the practice of everyday virtues such as patience, civility, honesty, wisdom, and justice. Communication, too—as for all good friends—is always important.

Interchurch couples often have much to learn about each other's Christian tradition. Learning not only includes each tradition's particular take on church doctrine, but the personal practices that make that faith come alive in worship, in family life, and in the community. All the understandings and emotions attached to these particulars of Christian living can be shared with benefit for both partners, for we live out of both our heads and our hearts.

Thoughts and feelings often surface at Advent and Christmas, Lent, Holy Week, and Easter. These seasons—and the celebrations that mark them—present couples with opportunities for discussion and prayer. They represent occasions in which to seek together the guidance of the Spirit in the shaping of the couple's own ways of celebrating special feasts and events. The key here is to do more, rather than to reduce religious practices. Participation in joint religious activities can help couples grow together. Today, there are many opportunities such as ecumenical Bible studies or social action groups in which interchurch couples can live and deepen their Christian faith together.

Given that interchurch families look for ways to participate in the life of their two communities so that their own two-church gift may be recognized, respected, and welcomed, the American Association of Interchurch Families offers these suggestions for local congregations:

- Enter into mutual consultation between Christian pastors for supporting such marriages and upholding their values.
- Explore ways in which interchurch families can contribute positively to your church communities, and ways in which they can be nurtured as we journey towards deeper unity together.
- Conduct marriage preparation jointly, working together with other local churches.
- Because of the couples' mutual responsibility, pastoral care that concerns both partners or their children should be exercised with both of them present and, when appropriate, their children, and not exercised through just one of the partners as intermediary.
- In the work of raising children, respect the conscientious decisions made by the parents together, recognizing that the unity of the marriage is paramount.
- As far as possible, mark major stages in life such as baptism, profession of faith, or confirmation as ecumenical events in which both churches play at least some recognizable part.
- Hold shared services in which interchurch families can give public thanks for the birth of their children, pray for their upbringing in the life of their two church communities, and dedicate themselves anew to God for this purpose.[17]

Fr. George Kilcourse, who was largely responsible for getting the American Association started and who continues to guide the Association and its Board of Directors, composed these beatitudes for a presentation he made in California in 1997:

Blessed are the interchurch spouses who participate also in the church of their partners from another Christian tradition; theirs is the Kingdom of God.

Blessed are the interchurch parents who share fully together in the religious education of their children; such children will grow to see the unity of the Body of Christ.

Blessed are the sorrowing interchurch families who have not found pastors to accept and minister to their needs; they will be comforted.

Blessed are the merciful interchurch couples who patiently work with their pastors and help to awaken them to Christ's presence in their marriage; they will know mercy.

Blessed are the interchurch spouses who are pure of heart; their marriage will be recognized as a sacrament of Christ.

Blessed are the interchurch couples who minister to engaged and newly married interchurch couples; on them God's favor rests.

Blessed are the interchurch families who hunger and thirst for the unity of the Body of Christ; they will be satisfied.

Blessed are interchurch spouses when they persecute you and utter all kinds of slander against you because you have married a Christian from another tradition; you will be called daughters and sons of God.[18]

Those in interchurch marriages clearly bring to the church, by the testimony of their love and their vows, a call to all of us to continue to respond to the Holy Spirit's present gift of unity and to collaborate with the Spirit and one another in the journey to full unity of the church.

5. MONASTICS, RELIGIOUS COMMUNITIES, AND LAY MOVEMENTS

Not only every person but every group has a contribution to make to the unity of Christ's church. We all carry a piece of colored glass to place in the mosaic of unity the Holy Spirit is in the process of creating. In this chapter, we will look at what monastic and religious communities, societies of apostolic life, and lay movements can do to make a difference.

The *Directory for the Application of Principles and Norms on Ecumenism* has a section that focuses specifically on the contribution to be made by these groups:

Institutes of Consecrated Life and Societies of Apostolic Life

While the concern for restoring Christian unity involves the whole Church, clergy and laity alike, religious orders and congregations and societies of apostolic life, by the very nature of their particular commitments in the Church and the contexts in which they live out these commitments, have significant opportunities of fostering ecumenical thought and action. In accordance with their particular charisms and constitutions—some of which antedate the divisions among Christians—and in the light of the spirit and aims of their institutes, they are encouraged to put into practice, within the concrete possibilities and limits of their rules of life, the following attitudes and activities:

a) to foster an awareness of the ecumenical importance of their particular forms of life in as much as conversion of heart, personal holiness, public and private prayer and service to the Church and the world are at the heart of the ecumenical movement;

b) to contribute to an understanding of the ecumenical dimensions of the vocation of all Christians to holiness of life by offering occasions for developing spiritual formation, contemplation, adoration and praise of God and service to one's neighbor;

c) taking account of the circumstances of place and persons, to organize meetings among Christians of various Churches and ecclesial Communities for liturgical prayer, for recollection and spiritual exercises, and for a more profound understanding of Christian spiritual traditions;

d) to maintain relations with monasteries or communities of common life in other Christian Communions for an exchange of spiritual and intellectual resources, and experiences in apostolic life, since the growth of the religious charisms in these Communions can be a positive factor for the whole of the ecumenical movement. This can provide a fruitful spiritual emulation;

e) to conduct their many varied educational institutions with a view to ecumenical activity;

f) to collaborate with other Christians in the areas of common work for social justice, economic development, progress in health and education, the safeguarding of creation, and for peace and reconciliation among nations and communities;

g) insofar as religious conditions permit, ecumenical action should be encouraged, so that, "while avoiding every form of indifferentism, or confusion and also senseless rivalry, Catholics might collaborate with their separated brethren, insofar as it is possible, by a common profession before the nations of faith in God and in Jesus Christ, and by a common, fraternal effort in social, cultural, technical and religious matters, in accordance with the Decree on Ecumenism. Let them cooperate, especially, because of Christ their common Lord. May his Name unite them!"[1]

The directory then goes on to indicate that in these activities, religious communities and lay movements will observe the norms for ecumenical work that have been established by the diocesan bishop, the synods of Eastern Catholic Churches or Episcopal Conferences, as an expression of their cooperation in the total apostolate within a given territory. They are encouraged as well to maintain close contacts with the various diocesan or national ecumenical commissions. The directory then recommends putting an office or a commission in place to ensure that they hold their focus and stay committed to the task of fostering unity in every way they can among the followers of Jesus.

> To assist this ecumenical activity, it is very opportune that the various institutes of consecrated life and societies of apostolic life establish, on the level of their central authorities, a delegate or a commission charged with promoting and assisting their ecumenical engagement. The function of these delegates or commissions will be to encourage the ecumenical formation of all the members, aid the specific ecumenical formation of those who have particular offices and act as advisors for ecumenical affairs to the various general and local authorities of the institutes and societies, especially for initiating or carrying forward the activities described above (n. 51).[2]

Following the Second Vatican Council, all the religious orders and institutes in the church were called to renew their life and mission in the light of their founder's vision. For my own community, that occasioned a dramatic shift in the understanding of our mission.

The Missionary Society of St. Paul the Apostle, more popularly known as the Paulist Fathers, was founded in 1858 by Isaac Thomas Hecker, a convert from evangelical Methodism, and three companions, all former Episcopalians, who had entered the Catholic Church through the Oxford Movement. A fifth original member, also a convert, left the Paulist community over Hecker's insistence that their primary work would be to use the means of the age to work for the conversion of Protestant America.[3]

Conversion from one form of Christianity to another was quite common in nineteenth-century America and was seen as the principal means to bring about the unity of Christians. Toward the end of his life, Hecker would promote values inherent in what are today the fundamentals of post–Vatican II dialogue. He wrote that religious people of his age sought unity and that dialogue among them was a positive and productive task. Hecker believed that the present divisions between Christians hampered efforts to evangelize the world and he advocated for the search for Christian teaching held in common. "Let us cultivate the things that make for unity," he wrote.[4]

The transformation of the Catholic Church's view on Christian unity from before the Council to now has been one of the greatest examples of organizational conversion in the history of the world.[5] The promotion of Christian unity was one of the two formal reasons Pope John XXIII convoked the Council, the other being the reform and renewal of the Catholic Church, which, he said, was the best way the Catholic Church could contribute to the reunion of Christians. In the end, both reasons were related to unity among the followers of Jesus.

The Council had a profound impact on the Paulist community. For one hundred years, Paulists had identified themselves as missionaries and as experts on bringing members of other churches into the Catholic Church. After the Council, while the goal of Christian unity remained the same, the model and means underwent dramatic change. The missionary outreach was differently framed. Conversion was now carefully directed to the unchurched and the lapsed, and not to other practicing Christians. The ministry model where Protestants were concerned was now dialogue and collaboration on campus, between local congregations, and in downtown Catholic Information Centers.

In 1986, after a twenty-year period of experimentation in new forms of ministry, the community's highest governing body issued a Mission Direction Statement defining the Paulist mission in terms of Evangelization, Reconciliation, and Ecumenism (later expanding that at the 2002 General Assembly to include a fourth orientation: Interreligious Relations). And in 1998, the Assembly moved to create a Paulist North American Office for Ecumenical and Interfaith Relations, now located in Washington, DC.

In those intervening years, Paulists served on the Vatican Secretariat for Promoting Christian Unity (now the Pontifical Council for Promoting Christian Unity), directed the international Tantur Ecumenical Institute in Jerusalem, the Canadian Centre for Ecumenism, served in the ecumenical offices of the Conference of Catholic Bishops in both the United States and Canada, as well as in the role of diocesan ecumenical officers.

The Paulists are by no means the only religious communities that carry the Catholic Church's mission for unity among Christians in high profile. The Graymoor Ecumenical and Interreligious Institute is a ministry of the Franciscan Friars of the Atonement, a Roman Catholic religious community of brothers and priests in the tradition of St. Francis of Assisi. The founder of the Society of the Atonement, Fr. Paul Wattson, SA, was an early pioneer of the ecumenical movement in the United States. From his friary at Graymoor, in Garrison, New York, he contributed to the founding of what is now the Week of Prayer for Christian Unity and identified the primary work of the Friars of the Atonement to be that of Christian unity.

The Glenmary Home Missioners, a community founded in 1939 by Fr. William Howard Bishop to work in the rural United States among the Catholic minority in Appalachia and the South, have opened an office for Catholic-Evangelical Relations. In an astute use of the social media to further their apostolate by connecting with people online, they began by launching a Facebook fan page. Alluding to the hymn "They will know we are Christians by our Love," it's simply called, They Will Know. "Our aim is to increase understanding between Catholics and Evangelicals, support interchurch couples, raise awareness of the topical issues impacting our common faith, and to promote spiritual growth. In addition to launching a web site, down the road we hope to develop this ministry in partnership with an Evangelical organization. In this way we'll be able to expand the reach as well as the credibility of this truly valuable ministry."[6]

The Jesuits have held an International Congress of Jesuit Ecumenists about every two years since Vatican II. There is a secretariat for ecumenical and interreligious relations in the Jesuit curia in Rome. The United States Jesuit Conference also put in place an advisory board on interreligious relations and ecumenical dialogue.

Other examples could be given, but these suffice to illustrate the point: religious communities and communities of apostolic life can make a valuable contribution to the work for Christian unity. And while these institutional expressions are positive signs of commitment to that work, in the end, of course, what it really comes down to is this: How many of the members of all these communities take every opportunity to join hands in mission, prayer, and service with members of other churches?

The American Methodist theologian and church historian Albert Outler was an official observer at the Second Vatican Council. The words he reportedly addressed to leaders of religious communities in the Catholic Church need to be heard again today. He challenged them and the members of their communities to take up the ecumenical cause once more and make it their own, "not because you are vowed to unity more than other Christians, but because you are vowed to holiness."

"My plea," said Outler, "is that in your zeal for God's reign you should never ease the cause of Christian unity over to the margins of your commitments, never rank it as a deferred priority, never rest content with the ecumenical *status quo*, which is still a scandal—in God's eyes and even in the eyes of the world."[7]

THE CONTRIBUTION OF MONASTIC COMMUNITIES

One might think that monasteries, given their usually isolated locations and the reclusive lifestyle of their inhabitant monks, would simply be "off the screen" in terms of potential contributions to the church's mission for unity. In a lecture given in 1999 at the symposium "Monastic Life and Religious Experience from the Nineteenth to the Twentieth Century,"[8] the founder of a new monastery (1965) in northwestern Italy, Enzo Bianchi, shared three reasons why monastic life provides a particularly ecumenical terrain.

First, monasticism precedes the divisions in the church. It is a human phenomenon with its own anthropology (celibacy, community life or solitude, asceticism, the search for the absolute) even before it became a Christian phenomenon. It is for this reason that interreligious dialogue (such as the North American Monastic Buddhist-Catholic Dialogue) takes place in monasteries more than elsewhere.

Further, within Christianity, as long as the churches remained united, monasticism remained single and undivided, with its Western expression recognizing the Eastern monasticism of the desert fathers as its source. Thus, every monastic ought to see that the undivided church is his or her true home.

Secondly, monasticism came into being as a radical commitment to follow Christ and, therefore, as a pathway to holiness. When holiness is pursued in religious life, even in different churches, it is a unifying force. Holiness allows us to realize that confessional walls do not rise as high as heaven. It was the French priest Abbé Paul Couturier—the same one who helped shape what we presently call the Week of Prayer for Christian Unity—who said that at a certain degree of holiness, confessional differences lose their force because holiness looks beyond the division of the churches.

If monastics truly respond to their vocation of inner unification, communion lived visibly, and continually renewed reconciliation and mercy, says Bianchi, they will be servants of unity and ministers of ecclesial communion.

A third reason that makes monasticism a natural site for ecumenical dialogue is that it has always sought to be a life of conversion. As the dictum goes, "the church is always reforming itself." But in the history of the church, concrete expressions of reform have been few, and what reform there is tends to be put into effect slowly. In monastic life, on the other hand, every century has seen a reform in which there has been an effort to return to the sources and begin again, in a more profound obedience and faithfulness to the gospel. Because of the centrality of the word of God in monastic life—the Office, *lectio divina*, Eucharist—and the resulting emphasis on reform, monasticism is capable of speaking the same language as the Reformed Churches and of being their authentic dialogue partner.

"We must confess, though," says Bianchi, "that many monastic and religious communities simply do not investigate the ecumenical pathway toward reconciliation: they consider ecumenical activity optional, or they think of it as a specific charism granted ecumenical communities. As a result, they plan and organize their way of life, their *diakonia*, and their mission in society among the churches without taking into consideration the other Christian traditions."[9]

TAIZÉ AND MONASTICISM'S PROTESTANT RECLAMATION

If you think of monasticism as a Catholic and Eastern Orthodox expression of Christian life, but absent from Protestantism, think again. In Europe, since World War II, monasticism has been slowly filtering back into the Protestant experience among both men and women.

Taizé, in the south of Burgundy, France, is the home of an international, ecumenical community, founded in 1940 by Brother Roger Schütz. Son of a Swiss Calvinist pastor and French Protestant mother, Roger was the youngest child in the family with seven sisters. Raised with a rigorous Protestantism, Roger's parents allowed him nonetheless, at age thirteen, to stay with a Catholic, Madame Biolley, while pursuing his studies in a nearby town. Their conversations awakened in him an ecumenical vocation at a young age.

His father eventually directed him toward studies in theology at the University of Lausanne, where he was elected as president of the student Christian association. In the Reformation era, both Luther and Calvin basically did away with monasticism as an expression of Christian life, but Roger was clearly looking at things with a fresh eye. He wrote his thesis on the ideal of the monastic life according to St. Benedict and its conformity to the gospel.

In 1940, at the outbreak of the Second World War, he left Switzerland for the region of Burgundy in France in which his mother grew up. While visiting the ruins of the famous monastery of Cluny, razed during the Reform, he saw in the village of Cluny a notice in the window of the local barrister of a "House for sale at Taizé," ten kilometers away.

There he settled and began welcoming political refugees, mostly Jews, whom the war had compelled into exile. After two years of living on meager resources, he was betrayed to the Vichy police, and only in 1944 was he able to return to the village of Taizé. However, during his exile in Geneva, a few young men had already joined him. They took as their own a simple rule of life that Roger had found and that the monastic community of Cluny had adopted several years before: "Throughout your day let work and rest be quickened by the Word of God. Keep inner silence in all things and you will dwell in Christ. Be filled with the spirit of the beatitudes: joy, simplicity, mercy."[10]

At the time of the Liberation, in a crippled France, the first brothers of Taizé were struck by the suffering of the German prisoners who were being held in camps nearby. They soon received authorization to welcome these prisoners for a meal once a week. In the simple and deeply human hospitality that was extended, a gospel reality was sown that would come to mark the life of their community: reconciliation.

The first seven brothers committed themselves on Easter Day in 1949 to celibacy and community life lived in great simplicity. In the silence of a long retreat in 1952–53, Brother Roger wrote the Rule of Taizé. Monasticism was slowly re-entering the bloodstream of European Reform-Church Protestantism.

Brother Roger had in mind a small community of no more than fifteen. All of its first members were Protestant. Not surprisingly, Catholics—both comfortable and familiar with this form of Christian living—began to present themselves as well. And so what has come to be called a "parable of community" and a "parable of reconciliation" began to take shape. The parable of Taizé: to show that the divided church remains the one church. To the diversity of the various Christian denominations was added the diversity of nations. Today, of the hundred or so brothers who form the community, approximately thirty countries and all continents are represented. Brother Roger once said in an interview on the community's development,

> When I was young, I was astonished to see Christians talking about a God of love while at the same time wasting so much energy in justifying oppositions. And I said to myself: To communicate Christ, is there anything more transparent than a life that is given, a life where day after day reconciliation is accomplished concretely?
>
> Since then, this intuition has never left me: a life in community could be a sign that God is love. Little by little, the conviction grew within me that it was essential to

create a community with men who would give their whole life, and who would seek to understand each other and to live continually in communion; a community where goodness of heart and simplicity would be at the center of everything.

It is urgent to do all we can so that a new breath of communion spreads out as far as possible. It is fundamental for Christians to enter on the way opened by Christ when he says: "Go first and be reconciled" (Matt 5:24). "Go first!," not: "Put it off until later."[11]

THE COMMUNITY'S DEVELOPMENT

The aroma of authentic gospel living went out, and people began to come. Already by the end of the 1950s, young people were finding their way to Taizé in increasing numbers. Since 1962, brothers and young people sent by Taizé began to come and go quietly and with discretion in the countries of Eastern Europe. In the West, Brother Roger saw that the political activism of the late 1960s among youth did not go deep enough. On the one hand, young people were fleeing institutions, deserting parishes and movements; and on the other, they demonstrated a thirst for God, friendship, and a quest for purpose in life.

In 1970 at Easter, with 2,500 young adults present, Brother Roger called for a Council of Youth that was launched four years later with 50,000 participants. Since then, Taizé has also played a key role in terms of grassroots organization for the World Youth Days, and its International Meetings, which are held between Christmas and New Year in different European countries, have drawn up to 100,000 people from around the world.

One can only be amazed. Here, on a hilltop in the countryside outside a village so small it is not even on most maps of France, is this community that has no confessional identity, no canonical status or juridical constitution. It is not trying to corral anyone. It is not a church and it even resists becoming a movement. It only wants to be a sign of the church and a way into it. It only wants to witness to the one church that is the bedrock of all the churches. It just wants to say that unity is not something to be built but something to be discovered. It simply seeks to embrace the gospel and live its essential message that we are reconciled to God and to one another through the life, death, and resurrection of Jesus. Its message to those from different races, cultures, languages, and denominations is simply this: come and see. Christ destroys every separating wall.

In his Letter for the European Youth Meeting in Milan in 1998, Brother Roger wrote, "Without reconciliation, what future is there for this unique communion of love called 'Church'? Ecumenism becomes immobile when it creates parallels which do not become joined and which ends by exhausting the resources of energy for reconciliation. It is like two trains traveling on parallel tracks. From time to time they stop and allow an encounter and then everyone gets back on their own train. When the ecumenical vocation does not concretize itself in reconciliation, it goes nowhere and the flame is extinguished."[12]

That daily concretization of reconciliation in lived experience is what makes Taizé a parable of community. In a 2014 letter "Towards a New Solidarity," Brother Roger's successor, Brother Alois, made four proposals that represent a commitment to "seeking visible communion with all who love Christ": (1) Join a local praying community; (2) Extend friendship beyond the boundaries that limit us; (3) Share and pray regularly with others; and (4) Make the communion among all who love Christ more visible. And he ends his letter with a suggestion for local pastoral leaders: "In pastoral work, do together with Christians of other denominations all that can be done together; do nothing without taking others into account."[13]

GRANDCHAMP

In the 1930s, a few women in the Reformed Church in French-speaking Switzerland were rediscovering the importance of silence for their life of faith. They organized a spiritual retreat, at first once a year, in a house at Grandchamp outside of Neuchâtel. In the course of time, retreats became more frequent and were opened up to other people.

Soon the need was felt to keep the house open throughout the year and to provide for the continual presence of prayer. The first sisters, rooting their lives in meditation on the word of God, rediscovered the stream of monastic life through the friendship and support of Catholic, Anglican, and Orthodox communities. A commitment to prayer for the unity of the church marks them from their origins.

In 1952, the first sisters committed themselves to leave everything behind and follow Christ on the way of the Beatitudes, to be together a sign of the coming kingdom, a place of reconciliation, of communion, and of praise. Shortly thereafter, they adopted the Rule of Taizé and its daily Offices as the basis for their life in community and liturgical prayer.

The community drew from both the Catholic and Orthodox traditions in its prayer life, with a regular celebration of the Eucharist (twice weekly) and Eastern musical tonalities, icons, and the Jesus Prayer, so dear to the Christian East: Lord Jesus Christ, Son of the Living God, have mercy on me, a sinner.

Today, the Community comprises about sixty sisters, coming from different Protestant Churches and from various countries. The majority of the sisters live at Grandchamp, near Neuchâtel, while others live in small communities of two or three at various locations in Switzerland, Israel, Algeria, France, and elsewhere. There they seek to be simply a presence of friendship and prayer. Together with the members of the Order of Unity (men and women who live out their calling to Christian unity within their family, parish, and professional realities) and with the Servants of Unity (women who live consecrated lives in the monastic spirit, but remain in the world), the Community is gathered into a great family, all who share a common spirituality.[14]

Hospitality is extended to all those looking to find meaning in their life—Christians of all confessions, Jews, Muslims, and believers of other faiths. The sisters seek to make their home a place of welcome, dialogue, and encounter for all. In the words of Sr. Françoise, one of the community's members:

> The Community seeks to share the heart of its vocation with all those we receive—prayer, the search for Christian unity, a common life shared in friendship and simplicity of lifestyle. Together we strive to be a sign of the coming kingdom, of the compassion of God, and to make our home a place of reconciliation, healing and hope for the church and the world. Our vocation to the *monos* (Greek,

meaning "one" from which "monk" derives) deepens, widens, and leads us always back to our essential oneness or unity. Unity is at the very heart of our spiritual quest. It begins in our own person and widens out to become that "passionate concern for the unity of the Body of Christ" of which the Rule of Taizé speaks.[15]

BOSE

The monastic community of Bose in northwestern Italy came into being on December 8, 1965—the day the Second Vatican Council concluded its work. The founder, Enzio Bianchi, a Catholic layman, began living in a rented house near the dairy farms at Bose. Among the first three people to join him was a Protestant pastor and a Catholic laywoman. Today, community members call it "the gift of our origin" and see the Holy Spirit's work in the fact that among the earliest members, there was both male and female, Protestant and Catholic.

The monastic community at Bose presently numbers about eighty—approximately fifty men and thirty-five women. Only a half dozen or so among them are ordained, giving a strong emphasis to the call to holiness among laity. Only a few among them are Protestants, best explained perhaps by the history of Italian Protestantism and its harsh struggle for survival in a dominantly Catholic country, but the community self-identifies as "a monastic community of men and women belonging to different churches."[16]

The community recognizes its roots in the local Catholic Church and carries out a typically ecclesiastical ministry both in its own diocese and in other local churches: preaching, spiritual retreats, the publication of studies, books, and articles on spirituality. Bianchi himself is an increasingly sought-after commentator on events in the church and world.

When the community members come into chapel in their white robes for one of their three daily Offices, one is first struck by how young they are (the median age in the community, according to one member, is about thirty-nine). But when they take their places in the choir (men on the left, women on the right), first bowing toward the altar and then coming erect and facing one another, something else emerges. As they chant the psalms—the men singing the first two verses of each stanza and the women the last two—a powerful image of the complementarity of men and women in the church emerges both visually and audibly.

In an effort to listen, to understand, and to serve other churches, the community has organized each year since 1993 an international ecumenical conference on Russian spirituality. The conference takes place at Bose every September and offers Eastern Orthodox and Western Christian scholars the chance to meet one another and seek a deeper communion among the churches through an exploration of the spiritual treasures of their respective traditions.

In a similar spirit, in 1996, the community began organizing a series of conferences on Protestant spirituality, in collaboration with the Protestant universities of Neuchâtel (Switzerland) and Strasbourg (France). Bianchi points to a prophetic horizon for forms of religious life wherein Christians of different denominations share life together. He knows from personal experience that this requires a great deal of courage, evangelical boldness, mutual submission, and an ability to leave behind the confessional traditions and practices that are not essential to the following of Christ, and a willingness to go the extra mile.

> Finally, it will not happen without an inner fire, a passion for communion that pushes us forward in our search for unity in diversity, and that allows us to look ahead and glimpse the unity toward which we must travel together....Here and there interdenominational monastic life is beginning to reveal the new ways in which ecumenism is becoming, once again, a prophecy within monasticism. Some Christians are living together and sharing the same vocation and the same ministry, even though the churches to which they belong do not yet live in visible communion.
>
> Monasticism and ecumenism can no longer be understood apart from each other. In the journey toward reconciliation among the churches, monasticism plays a particularly important role, because it permits a common life in which it is possible to live together reconciled, working patiently toward full unity in a church of churches able to recognize one another in a single confession of faith.[17]

THE NEW MONASTICS

What's happening in North America? In 2008, the *Boston Globe* reported on the rise of the New Monastics in North America. Some one hundred groups that describe themselves as both evangelical and monastic have sprung up largely since the turn of the new millennium. They come from a variety of Protestant traditions—from Presbyterian to Pentecostal—and share a common dissatisfaction with what they see as the over-commercialized and socially apathetic culture of mainstream evangelicalism, especially in its "prosperity gospel" expression.[18]

Both Luther and Calvin removed monasticism from the range of legitimate forms of Christian living. True Christians, according to the sixteenth-century reformers, were to be engaged with the world, not spending their time chanting in Latin. However, today, increasing numbers of evangelical congregations have created relationships with Catholic monasteries and have joined the monks for spiritual retreats. St. John's Abbey, a Benedictine monastery in Minnesota, now makes a point of including interested evangelicals in its summer Monastic Institute.

"I grew up in a tradition that believes Catholics are pagans," said Zach Roberts, founder of the Dogwood Abbey in Winston-Salem, North Carolina, who was raised Southern Baptist and serves as a pastor in a Baptist Church. "I never really understood that. Now I'd argue against that wholeheartedly."[19] He meets regularly with a Trappist monk to talk about how to contemplate God.

These mostly young, single Christians are turning to an ancient tradition to provide spiritual sustenance for their ministries. They are discovering prayer and study as ways of engaging with and for the world, but they are not stopping there. The new monasticism that is evolving does not aim to separate itself from society, but rather is environmentally conscious and cares about social justice.

They see their simple living, grounded in prayer and service, as a way to better integrate core Christian values into their lives as contemporary citizens. They see in community life an answer to society's materialism and the church's complacency toward it. They see the new monasticism responding to and providing a space for community, love, and intimacy. They seek intimacy with Jesus and a life of uncompromising adherence to his predilection for those on the margins of society as expressed in his Sermon on the Mount. Scott Bessenecker, director of global projects for InterVarsity Christian Fellowship, says that he sees "an emerging movement of youth taking up residence in slum communities in the same spirit that I find in the start of the Franciscans and the early Celtic orders and in the Jesuits."[20]

In 2004 a conference in Durham, North Carolina, marked the birth of the new monasticism and brought together older communities like the Mennonite Reba Place Fellowship, Bruderhof, and the Catholic Worker, along with fourteen newer communities from across the United States. Participants wrote a voluntary rule and developed twelve "distinctives" that would mark their communities, including submission to the larger church, living with the poor and outcast, living near community members, hospitality, nurturing a common community life and a shared economy, peacemaking, reconciliation, care for creation, celibacy or monogamous marriage, novitiate formation of new members, and contemplation.[21] A fruit flowing from the conference was the book *Schools for Conversion: 12 Marks of a New Monasticism*,[22] representing a communal attempt to discern the marks of a new monasticism in the inner cities and forgotten landscapes of the empire that is called America.

"We've lost the art of vow-making," Bessenecker states. "In a community that has become so connected to their iPods and gaming, calling people to something different is the sort of challenge they're ready to rise to....A community of single people can represent God's expanded view of the family, that we are all brothers and sisters in Christ." Though the new monasticism is a minority movement, Bessenecker says its impact could be far beyond the numbers of people involved. "None of these historical movements were ever a huge percentage of the Christian population," he said. "But they had a disproportionate impact on society. I think we're going to see that in the next 50 years."[23]

LAY MOVEMENTS AND INSTITUTES OF CONSECRATED LIFE

There are persistent, historical questions relating to our understanding of the church, sacraments, ministry, and a way of making decisions in the church that would be acceptable to all. But the Holy Spirit keeps finding a way to move the churches forward. When one looks at the big picture, there is positive energy circulating that is bringing people from different traditions together in exciting ways. Another shining example of this in the European context is "Together for Europe," a network of relationships among movements and new communities that is geared toward promoting reconciliation, peace, and solidarity in the European continent.

It traces its origins back to the historical meeting of the movements and communities called by Pope John Paul II in 1998 that brought together 400,000 people in St. Peter's Square. "Together for Europe" was launched in 1999 in Ottmaring, Germany. Here, leaders of the Evangelical Lutheran and Catholic movements met together on the same day of the signing by Vatican and Lutheran World Federation authorities of the Joint Declaration on the Doctrine of Justification.

Things began to gather momentum and the Holy Spirit was at work building relationships across the denominations. In 2004, the first "Together for Europe" event was held in Stuttgart, Germany, drawing together nine thousand participants. Here, representatives of over 170 movements sealed their commitment stating that, inspired by the transforming power of the gospel, they felt called to work for a continent that is multifaceted and united. This first step was broadened in 2007 with Stuttgart II, where 250 communities and movements took an even bigger step of solidarity. They committed themselves to continue the journey together with seven specific goals, saying yes to life, family, creation, a just economy, solidarity, peace, and social responsibility.

In 2012, they responded to the call by going right to the heart of Europe and holding an event close to the European parliament in Brussels. Their intention was to speak to politicians about their call and commitment to revive the Christian soul of the European continent. Representatives of three hundred movements came together from a variety of backgrounds: Orthodox, Lutherans, Catholics, Reformed, Anglicans, Methodists, and Free Churches. The event was also broadcasted by satellite to 130 cities across Europe where local events were being held.

Maria Voce, the president of the Focolare movement, spoke about "Together for Europe" as a seed of hope that, despite our different places of origin and histories, we have become friends and are connected by a fraternal collaboration. She highlighted that the root cause of many difficulties in Europe was fundamentally connected to a crisis of relationships. She called participants to come out from their individualism and intensify their relationship with every person that they encounter, basing it on the gospel and working toward a Europe concerned not only with people's material needs, but also with their moral, social, spiritual, and religious needs.[24]

A few months after the Stuttgart II gathering, Cardinal Walter Kasper, then head of the Council for the Promotion of Christian Unity, referred to the event in Stuttgart as one of the encouraging signs for Christian unity efforts today. "We can say that ecumenism is returning to its origins in small groups of dialogue, prayer and Bible study. Recently, these groups have also taken the word publicly, for example, in the large gatherings of movements at Stuttgart in 2004 and 2007. Hence, in addition to the official dialogue, which is often more difficult, there emerges new and promising forms of dialogue."[25]

In many cases, these movements and communities are not merely coming together in an international event as members of different churches, but they are either ecumenical in their internal composition or have a pronounced ecumenical sensitivity in their life and work.

What are some of these movements and communities? Here is a brief synopsis of a few of them.

FOCOLARE MOVEMENT

Whenever Chiara Lubich, a Catholic laywoman and founder of the Focolare Movement, would be asked to define its spirituality, she would respond with one word: *unity*. She liked to tell the story of how, in the middle of World War II in Trent, Italy, she and a few other girls were in an air-raid shelter reading the seventeenth chapter of John's Gospel—Jesus' last will and testament—by the light of a candle. When they came upon the words, "May they all be one, Father, as you and I are one," the words seemed to light up. That "all" expanded their horizon.

After a little while, when we became aware of the difficulty, if not the impossibility, of carrying out such a program, we felt urged to ask Jesus for the grace of teaching
us how to live unity. Kneeling around an altar we offered
our lives to him so that, if he wished, he could bring
about unity....In our hearts one thing was clear: unity is
what God wants from us. We live to be one with him
and one among ourselves and with everybody. This marvelous vocation binds us to heaven and immerses us in a
universal family. Nothing could be greater. For us, no
ideal excels this. That project for unity was to be the
goal of our life. Unity is the word that summarizes our
spirituality.[26]

Soon afterward that small group of people became a movement
that brought about a spiritual and social renewal. The movement
grew and developed through this spirituality that over time has
become a lifestyle for people of all ages, backgrounds, vocations, and
cultures. At its heart are the Focolare Centers, small communities of
men or women, single and married.

In this age of dramatic change, in sharing with humanity the
painful birth of a new civilization that is globalized, interdependent,
multicultural, and multifaith, the Focolare Movement is committed,
together with many other forces that are moving in this direction, to
build the unity of the human family enriched by diversity.

In 1961, Chiara founded the Focolare secretariat for ecumenism called "Centro Uno" (One Center) in Rome. Gabriella
Fallacara, codirector of Centro Uno, explained its work relating to a
"dialogue of life" and a "dialogue of the people." Everyone is called
to live this dialogue, not just the experts:

It is a fruit of the spirituality being lived out together by
Christians of different churches. By living the Gospel
together we can discover how great is the wealth of our
common patrimony: our baptism, the Scriptures, the first
Councils, the Creed, the Fathers of the Church and the
martyrs. Life together has made us more aware of these
bonds that already unite us.

Our common baptism is the sacramental bond of unity. The presence of Jesus in the midst of his people leads, encourages us and makes us brothers and sisters who bear different gifts that each can share. It is a true and original exchange of gifts that shine forth from the dialogue of life.[27]

Laypeople, priests, ministers, and bishops are all a part of it, both the grassroots and the leadership, making it a dialogue of all the people who are part of the Mystical Body of Christ. In less than 60 years of life, the movement has spread worldwide to 182 countries. Focolare is "a people" presently numbering over 50,000 Christians of 350 different churches and ecclesial communities. Persons of every age, vocation, religion, conviction, and culture belong to the Focolare family.[28]

Its purpose: to work cooperatively to build a more united world, following the inspiration of Jesus' prayer to the Father "that they may all be one" (John 17:21), respecting and valuing diversity. It focuses on dialogue as a method, has a constant commitment to building bridges and relationships of fraternity among individuals, peoples, and cultural worlds.[29]

SYNDESMOS FELLOWSHIP

A significant development in Orthodoxy over the past fifty years has been the work of Syndesmos—the World Fellowship of Orthodox Youth. Syndesmos was founded in 1953 to encourage contacts among Orthodox youth movements in Western Europe, Greece, and the Middle East. Today, Syndesmos has grown into a federation of 121 youth movements and theological schools in 43 different countries around the world. At the heart of the Fellowship is the desire of young Orthodox to work together serving the unity, witness, and renewal of the church. Through Syndesmos, Orthodox young people have made a significant contribution to the revival of the Orthodox mission. They have supported ecumenical engagement, raised questions concerning Orthodox unity, deepened and strengthened ties between the Orthodox and the Oriental Orthodox (Coptic, Ethiopian, Armenian, Syrian, and Indian) Churches. Since 1992, Oriental Orthodox youth movements have joined Syndesmos as federated members, with their own vice-president.[30]

THE COMMUNITY OF SANT'EGIDIO

The Community of Sant'Egidio began in Rome in 1968 at the initiative of a young man, Andrea Riccardi, who was then less than twenty. He gathered a group of high school students, like himself, to listen to and practice the gospel. The first Christian communities in the Acts of the Apostles and Francis of Assisi were the primary reference points.

The Community is a "church public lay association," a movement of laypeople with now more than sixty thousand members, dedicated to evangelization and charity in more than seventy-three countries throughout the world. The Community has as its center the Roman Church of Sant'Egidio, from which the Community takes its name.

Its different communities, spread throughout the world, share the same spirituality and principles that characterize the way of Sant'Egidio: prayer, communicating the gospel, solidarity with the poor, the search for unity among Christians, and dialogue as a way of peace-building between the different world religions. The Community has been instrumental in organizing several international ecumenical and interreligious events in recent years.[31]

THE SWORD OF THE SPIRIT

The nature and aim of this community is expressed in its charter: "The Word of the Spirit is an international, ecumenical Christian body that has come together to strengthen the Christian life of its members and to be an instrument for the Lord to establish his reign in the world."[32]

Inaugurated in 1982 as a "community of disciples on mission," The Sword of the Spirit seeks to:

- proclaim the good news of Christ through direct evangelization;
- bring together Christians from different traditions and cultures for common mission;
- support parents in raising children with character and a clear sense of identity;
- help bridge the gaps of race, class, and culture; and

- work in cooperation with the churches to foster Christian renewal and promote unity.

The Sword of the Spirit is an ecumenical association comprising more than sixty-five communities in twenty-four countries, supporting and enabling ten thousand people in using their time, money, and resources to help their fellow human beings. Members belong to Catholic, Protestant, and Orthodox traditions.[33]

From the beginning, men and women within their ranks from various Christian traditions desired to join together in worship, fellowship, and service. At the same time, they desired to remain faithful to their denominations. From these two desires grew an ecumenical endeavor, which they refer to as "cooperative ecumenism." It proceeds on the presupposition that we do not have full agreement or full unity, and do not expect it for some time to come. It requires that we love one another as brothers and sisters even now, looking forward to the time when the Lord will make greater unity possible. In the meantime, cooperation, wherever possible, is called for. "Whatever builds up, that we will try to do....The spirit behind such an approach is to seek to lay down our lives for all those whom we recognize as true brothers and sisters in Christ, and with them to advance the cause of Christ."[34]

L'ARCHE FEDERATION

L'Arche was born in Trosly-Breuil, France, in 1964, when Jean Vanier and Fr. Thomas Philippe, both Roman Catholics, began living with a few people with mental disabilities. Its name, L'Arche (English: ark), refers to Noah's ark, which provided security for the endangered. Within a short time, those belonging to other Christian traditions came and were welcomed as assistants. The people with disabilities were also welcomed regardless of religious affiliation.

In 1970, a L'Arche community called Daybreak was opened in Canada near Toronto by two Anglicans, Steve and Ann Newroth. Later that same year, in Bangalore, India, Gabrielle Einsle, a Roman Catholic, welcomed Hindus and Muslims to begin with her the first community in India. Today, there are 145 member communities of L'Arche across 40 countries on 5 continents—independent entities united by a common vision and a shared mission. In terms of religious belonging, some communities are more homogeneous than others, but there is no uniform religious affiliation. That surprises and disconcerts certain groups and institutions, and it complicates dialogue with particular churches.

Strictly speaking, L'Arche is not a movement but a federation. The Federation seeks to foster solidarity among communities, ensure unity in diversity, establish the conditions for membership, and create conditions for trust, service, dialogue, and mutual support. L'Arche USA and L'Arche Canada are part of this International Federation of L'Arche communities across the world.

At the heart of L'Arche communities are relationships between people with and without intellectual and developmental disabilities. The former are identified as "core members" and the latter as "assistants." A respectful relationship between people who treat each other as an equal provides security and allows for growth, personal development, and freedom.

The spirituality of L'Arche is grounded in the belief that each person is unique and of sacred value, and that we experience God's love through mutual friendships in which the gifts and weaknesses of each person are recognized and accepted. Persons with intellectual and developmental disabilities, through their own vulnerability, often have a special gift for touching hearts and revealing to us our own humanness. L'Arche seeks to live the Beatitudes—Jesus' call in the Sermon on the Mount to be people of simplicity, gentleness, compassion, justice, and peace.[35]

Worship is an important moment in which the community members celebrate their unity; it nurtures their desire to live together. During the 1980s, I served as an ecumenical advisor to the L'Arche communities in North America as they struggled with questions like the following: How can we, as members of different churches, pray together in our daily life? How might our house chapels reflect the diversity of backgrounds from which our members come? Living together with members of diverse religious backgrounds opened their eyes as never before to the reality of our divided church.

The differing practices of the churches with reference to eucharistic hospitality has been a source of deep pain and suffering, both for the assistants and the core members, the latter having no possibility of understanding reasons of history and theology. It makes them yearn for the divisions among Christians to be healed. People with disabilities feel the need for community in a particularly urgent way. One of the most precious gifts offered by the core members is that they are calling people to unity. They also have gifts of the heart that our churches and other religious communities need.[36]

Commissions on Ecumenism have been established in L'Arche's various geographical zones. Their mandate is to reflect on the questions that arise in their communities, to create links with other ecumenical communities, and to dialogue regularly with the ecumenical offices of the national churches. Margaret O'Donnell, who served as the chairperson for the Commission for Ecumenism for the Americas, once said, "Our handicapped brothers and sisters have led us to recognize in our own hearts the thirst for unity that is within us. They have revealed to us our ecumenical vocation."[37]

SUMMARY

There are many more movements and communities that could be included here, such as Iona in Scotland, Corrymeela and Columbanus in Northern Ireland, and Maranatha and Omega in England, to cite but a few. Nevertheless, the brief study of those in this chapter makes one aware of the emergence of a new reality: the priority of Christian community over that of a purely doctrinal approach. These ecumenical communities make clear the reality that the mutual recognition of Christians as Christians is the precondition rather than the goal. The essence of it is something that happens in the souls of Christians toward one another. Our bonds with one another in the Body of Christ are being experienced and manifested in new ways. This deep and wide spiritual traffic is providing a new form of *koinonia*, of "fellowship." At the same time, a sense of calling accompanies the gift: to make this new bond visible and to speak the truth that comes from within it: we are all members of the one Body of Christ.[38]

This is precisely what the ecumenical communities and movements are doing. It is important to note that, rather than seeking to found a new church, their members are patiently seeking the renewal of the churches amongst which the bond has been formed. To be sure, there is a tension in it, the tension of restlessness, of a double loyalty—on the one hand to the vision of the ecumenical movement, and on the other to the spiritual, institutional, theological, and historical structure of the church to which one belongs. But we need people who call for boldness, imagination, and forward-looking hope in action. There is an impatience that gives up, and an impatience that builds up.[39]

Each of the communities, monasteries, institutes, federations, and movements noted above shows us ways of responding in concrete terms to the task at hand.

6. SOCIAL ACTION GROUPS

At the heart of this question is the relationship between the church and the world, and at the core of that relationship is the divine concern for the world expressed in the Old Testament in the election of the people of Israel out of and for the sake of "all the nations." In the self-understanding of the New Testament community of believers in Jesus Christ, the community of the Body of Christ is seen as a new form of the covenant among the nations—not replacing God's covenant with Israel, but related to it—and as the sign of the coming restoration. This position of the church determines its relationship of basic solidarity with the world in suffering and in hope. Its foundational conviction is that it is in the life of the world that the signs of the kingdom have to be made manifest and credible.[1]

The increasing globalization of the world's societies with its related challenges around racism, poverty, and the promotion of interreligious dialogue have made the unity of humankind a more pressing issue than ever. It calls for us to take a fresh look at the relation between the church and the world in line with the nature of the church's mission in the world, the relation between general human history and "the history of salvation," the relation of humankind and the kingdom of God. The church is to be the sacrament, the sign, of the unification of the whole of humankind in God. For the church, this implies an awareness of its character as a pilgrim people and a readiness to cooperate with many secular movements serving the same purpose of humanity.[2]

As many Protestants are discovering in their social studies today, the Catholic Church has had a strong and leading voice in this area since the late nineteenth century through papal encyclicals and other church documents relating to justice and peace, beginning with Pope Leo XIII's encyclical, Of New Things (1891), in response to the conditions faced by workers following the onset of the Industrial Revolution. Issues it addresses include unbridled capitalism, a living wage, the relationship between classes, and the preferential option for the poor. Ensuing popes addressed the situation of their time: Pope Pius X on labor and industrialization in After Forty Years (1931); Pope John XXIII on overcoming excessive inequalities in Mother and Teacher (1961), and on what is needed for peace in the world in Peace on Earth (1963); Pope Paul VI on a Christian approach to economic development in On the Development of Peoples (1967); Pope John Paul II On Human Work (1981), On Social Concern (1987), and on The Hundredth Year anniversary of Leo XIII's Of New Things, a fresh look at the issues raised in it; and Pope Benedict XVI on charitable activity and loving one's neighbor in God is Love (2005) and on a broad range of social issues including poverty, injustice, the arms race, technology, and environmental protection in Charity in Truth (2009).[3]

As rich as these encyclicals are, the range and depth of Vatican documents goes well beyond and includes the Second Vatican Council's decrees on The Joys and the Hopes (1965) and Human Dignity (1965)[4] as well as Pope Francis's apostolic exhortation The Joy of the Gospel (2013)[5] in which he addresses, among other things, the social inclusion of the poor, peace, and the spiritual motivation for the church's missionary action.

In this chapter, however, we will demonstrate that Catholics have by no means been the only Christians addressing these important social questions. Social action has been and is increasingly common ground for us as followers of the gospel. Let's examine briefly the history of the consciousness-raising of all Christians over the past century.

CHURCH AND WORLD, LIFE AND WORK

A major factor in the birthing process of the ecumenical movement since World War I has been the concern for peace and international order. A major spasm in the birthing process of the ecumenical movement was the concern for peace and international order after World War I. The idea of forming a worldwide movement of churches to work for peace and justice between the nations, though it had often been discussed by Christian peace movements before the war, moved to the top of the list of priorities after the war. The immense human and social catastrophe caused by the war brought many church leaders to realize that their national churches had not only done too little to prevent it, but had even too readily participated in it. At the end of the war, the churches started plans for a conference that would help work for a just and lasting peace and formulate a Christian response to the economic, social, and moral issues in the post-war world.[6]

The universal Christian Conference on Life and Work took place in Stockholm, Sweden, in 1925. The words *life* and *work* expressed the organizers' determination to set forth "the Christian way of life" as the "world's greatest need." The aim was "to formulate programmes and devise means...whereby the fatherhood of God and the brotherhood of all peoples will become more completely realized through the church of Christ." One of the most memorable lines from the Stockholm conference was its insight that "the world is too strong for a divided church."[7] Unfortunately, the conference participants themselves were deeply divided on how to relate the Christian hope for the kingdom of God to the church's responsibility for the world, and in the end, the conference failed to measure up to its expectations, forcing the movement to engage in deeper analysis of the world's social and spiritual situation.

During a three-year preparatory period before the next Life and Work conference, which took place in 1937 in Oxford, England, several pioneering theological-ethical studies reformulated for the Life and Work Movement its view of the church's role in society. These studies involved contributions from several hundred leading theological and lay thinkers of that period, including representatives of all the major denominational communities. The conference report on its central theme, "Church, Community and State" made the Life and Work Movement a leading force in the eventual formation in 1948 of the World Council of Churches (WCC) because it saw in the tumultuous social situation of the world the compelling reason for moving decisively toward a global, dynamic, and informed fellowship of churches. From this pioneering movement flows the contemporary ecumenical concern with the social issues of our time:

human rights, democracy, racism, economic justice, religious liberty, to mention but a few.[8]

JUSTICE, PEACE, AND THE INTEGRITY OF CREATION

Following the founding of the WCC, there were other bench-mark developments, among which were two that are particularly worthy of mention relative to this theme. At its assembly in Vancouver, Canada (1983), the Council said that "to engage member churches in a conciliar process of mutual commitment (covenant) to justice, peace and the integrity of creation should be a priority for World Council programmes." Observing that "never before have so many lived in the grip of deprivation and oppression," and against the backdrop of an intense military arms race, the assembly said that "the biblical vision of peace with justice for all is not one of several options for the followers of Christ but is an imperative for our times."[9]

In 1990, the WCC sponsored a World Convocation on Justice, Peace and the Integrity of Creation (JPIC) in Seoul, Korea. The phrase, *integrity of creation*, besides alluding to the damage being done to the environment and the threat posed to the survival of life, underlines that a theology of life focuses on all life and not just human life. The convocation made the following ten affirmations:

- the exercise of power as being accountable to God
- God's option for the poor
- the equal value of all races and peoples
- male and female as created in the image of God
- truth is at the foundation of a community of free people
- the peace of Jesus of Christ
- the creation as beloved of God
- the earth as the Lord's
- the dignity and commitment of the younger generation
- human rights as being given by God[10]

The participants at Seoul also entered into covenant regarding these four concrete issues:

- a just economic order and liberation from the bondage of foreign debt;
- the true security of all nations and people and a culture of nonviolence;
- building a culture that can live in harmony with creation's integrity and preserving the gift of the earth's atmosphere to nurture and sustain the world's life; and
- the eradication of racism and discrimination on all levels for all peoples and the dismantling of patterns of behavior that perpetuate the sin of racism.

The JPIC world convocation was an important stage on the road toward common and binding pronouncements and actions on the challenges we continue to face.[11]

One that is becoming increasingly urgent is climate change. Representatives of Catholic organizations voiced disappointment at the conclusion of a United Nations summit on climate change at the end of 2013, and they urged church leaders to do more to mobilize the public to act on behalf of the environment as there seems to be no real commitment in this area by either developed or developing countries. Orthodox Archbishop Seraphim of Zimbabwe and Angola told Catholic News Service that effective counter-measures are hampered by the Western countries that "seem happier to sell guns than help governments adapt to climate damage. We need our congregations and communities to show spiritual solidarity with victims of climate change by promoting a sense of the common good over narrow national interests."[12]

Among submissions to the summit, the World Health Organization estimated that climate change was already causing an additional 140,000 deaths annually and that the developing countries were bearing the brunt of it from floods, storms, and droughts. Frederick D'Souza, director of the Catholic Church's official development arm, Caritas India, in one of the world's most vulnerable countries, said, "Churches must present a compassionate face to the world, showing how the poor are being further marginalized by climate change. The Bible tells us that we're stewards of the resources God has given us and we must not allow them to be expropriated and misused."[13]

Although some pastors and bishops are helping in the struggle for climate justice, their work faces strong resistance and often places them in danger, given that powerful mining, oil, and forestry companies have their own agents as well as government and police links. If the call for climate justice from faith communities is to be effective, they need to stand together. As the saying goes, "United we stand, divided we fall."

A wonderful and unprecedented example of such standing together was given when Pope Francis's encyclical *Laudato Si'* (Praise Be to You) was presented in June 2015 to a large press conference at the Vatican. Metropolitan John Zizioulas of Pergamon, a representative of Patriarch Bartholomew I, leader of the Eastern Orthodox Church, spoke on its behalf:

> I believe the significance of the papal Encyclical *Laudato Si'* is not limited to the subject of ecology as such. I see in it an important ecumenical dimension in that it brings the divided Christians before a common task which they must face together. We live at a time in which our fundamental existential problems overwhelm our traditional divisions and relativize them almost to the point of extinction.... Pope Francis' Encyclical is a call to unity—unity in prayer for our environment, in the same Gospel of creation, in the conversion of our hearts and our lifestyles to respect and love everyone and everything given to us by God. We are thankful for that.

In an encyclical framed as a call to action, Pope Francis makes a plea for a radical transformation of politics, economics and individual lifestyles to confront environmental degradation and climate change. The basic idea is that, in order to love God, you have to love your fellow human beings and you have to love and care for the rest of creation.[14]

THE CREATIVE TENSION

Throughout these decades of work on social questions, there has been a persistent tension between those ecumenists who give priority to the gospel's social dimension, and those who place spiritual and ecclesial communion in the first rank of importance. Clearly, it's not either/or, but both/and. Ecumenism is not just shared advocacy on behalf of peace and justice or simply dialogues aimed at resolving theological differences. Ecumenism must of necessity include a host of subjects and activities. The ecumenical river is fed by multiple streams, including shared prayer, common curricula development, life together in community, and other themes we have developed in these pages. It is all of these things and more, not as parallel initiatives, but as integrated dimensions of a single movement. We must hold all of them together in tension and insist that others do the same.[15]

The 2006 Assembly of the World Council of Churches in Porto Alegre, Brazil, did exactly that in its theological statement "Called to Be the One Church."[16] It calls on us to integrate the different dimensions of ecumenism: the unity of the church and the unity of humanity; the renewal of spirituality and mission; work for justice, peace, and the integrity of creation; mutual respect and cooperation among world religions.

"Called to Be the One Church" was the fruit of the work of the WCC's Faith and Order Commission, which had earlier produced other helpful documents such as "Church and World: The Unity of the Church and the Renewal of Human Community."[17] The latter, in focusing particularly on issues of justice and on the challenge of a more complete and authentic community of women and men, strongly affirms that search for unity and world-directedness are inseparable. What takes place in the church refers back to the world and forward to its final redemption. The overarching perspective is one of faith in the coming kingdom and the church as a prophetic sign of it.[18]

The relation between justice and Christian unity should be obvious, but it is clearly not always so. To cite but one example, racism is a radical distortion of the Christian faith and has divided the followers of Christ as much as, if not more than, doctrinal differences around the sacraments or different understandings of justification. *All* humans are created in the image of God. The justice we seek is not merely the coexistence of separated communities, but a new community in which those who have been excluded have a place. A church that is truly united will be a witness for justice not only through what it *says*, but through the way its diverse members *live* with one another. It is a fellowship based on common convictions and called to common witness. As Michael Kinnamon writes, "those who know themselves bound together in Christ will try to express the mind of Christ in one faith, one ministry, one sacramental life, and *one obedience*. Shared ethical commitments are a significant and visible part of deepening fellowship."[19]

SERVING THOSE IN NEED

Early on in the ecumenical movement, the principle was formed that we should do all things together, except where deep difference requires that we act separately. However, for the most part, we act separately, except where extraordinary circumstances dictate that we should act together. The movement for Christian unity must make a difference in the way Christians live their lives in local communities; it is not simply an international phenomenon.

An inspiring example of what can happen when Christians in local communities join hands in mission is given by the Annandale Christian Community for Action, located in an area of Virginia just west of the District of Columbia.[20]

In 1967, Fred and Emily Ruffing organized a meeting with representatives of eight local churches to set up a day care center to provide assistance to the working poor. They marshaled support from the county and from local donors. They succeeded in meeting the need. The organization they founded—the Annandale Christian Community for Action (ACCA)—branched out into other activities, all under the banner of "doing what Jesus would do." Over time, the organization has grown from eight to its current membership of twenty-six churches: five United Methodist and Baptist; four Roman Catholic; three Presbyterian and Episcopalian; two Lutheran, Evangelical, and Latter Day Saints Churches.

Today ACCA is a church-related voluntary organization serving those in need in the Annandale/Bailey's Crossroads area, regardless of religion, race, or ethnic background.

The initial concentration on day care grew to address a host of other needs: providing emergency food, delivery of basic furniture, providing emergency financial assistance, transportation to medical appointments, Meals on Wheels, providing housing rehabilitation, and offering scholarships for disabled students pursuing higher education.

The day care center is now the ACCA Child Development Center (CDC), which provides developmental childcare and early education for almost two hundred infants, toddlers, and preschoolers. Except for the staff of CDC, all other services in ACCA's full range of activities are provided by some seven hundred volunteers who offer assistance to those in need.

The ACCA Pantry collects from churches, schools, community groups, and local businesses and delivers food and other necessities on an emergency basis to area households. ACCA's Emergency Assistance program handles financial emergencies such as payment for rent, utilities, prescription drugs, and minor car repairs for low-income families who have few resources to fall back on in a crisis. These ministries provide a safety net while the families recover stability.

The furniture ministry volunteers collect and distribute gently used furniture to needy recipients. Since 2000, they've touched the lives of eighteen thousand persons, impacting the quality of their home lives in an immediate manner. Volunteers from the transportation ministry provide rides to medical appointments, while Meals on Wheels volunteers deliver meals every weekday to elderly residents who cannot fend for themselves. As partners with another organization, Rebuilding Together, ACCA volunteers spend a Saturday in April repairing houses. More than 110 homes have been repaired or rehabilitated since 1990. The annual CROP Hunger Walk raises funds for Church World Service, a portion of which is returned to ACCA.

In all these services, assistance is provided regardless of ethnicity or religion. According to Deputy County Executive for Neighborhood and Community Services Patricia Harrison, "ACCA has long been an important partner in our efforts to ensure healthy child and youth development, prevent homelessness, build families, and mitigate the impacts of poverty. ACCA exemplifies the role of community and faith-based organizations."[21]

The ACCA model of a faith-based organization collaborating with county government has been duplicated in other areas of the county. It is a sterling example of the power of members from various

Christian churches working together to put Christ's words into action. To make it even more real for readers, here is an interview with a Catholic couple, Anne Marie and Norman Hicks, who have a long track record in ACCA services:

Question: How long have you been involved with ACCA, and how did you first get involved?

Anne Marie and Norman: We became involved in ACCA in the Fall of 1970, after returning from two years in Ghana and settling in Annandale. Anne Marie signed up as a volunteer as a result of an ACCA volunteer recruitment table at Queen of Apostles Church after Sunday Mass. Initially, Anne Marie volunteered to deliver Meals on Wheels to the homebound, and then became a member of the Family Emergency Committee, which continues to this day, forty-four years later. Norman subsequently also volunteered, initially in the housing ministry. Eventually, we worked in various ministries, including food pantry, family emergency, transportation, and housing. Anne Marie has served as both President and Vice-President of ACCA, and Chair of the Family Emergency Committee. She is presently Chair of the Scholarship Committee, which honors our founders, Fred and Emily Ruffing, by recognizing high school students who have overcome a disability. Norman has been President, Vice-President, Treasurer, and is currently Chair of the Finance Committee.

Question: What has kept you engaged in this work over all these years?

Anne Marie and Norman: ACCA personifies the Christian ethic: "Doing what Jesus would do." ACCA clearly makes a difference, meeting the needs of the poor who lack food, furniture, child care, and emergency financial needs. Knowing that you are having an impact on helping people, plus the opportunity to work with other dedicated people from different churches, is personally very rewarding and has kept us involved. Since very little of ACCA's funds go into administration or fundraising, we know that contributions made will be really effective. ACCA rents no office space, and does not pay a salary to any of the volunteers involved in human services.

Question: How has your involvement affected your regard of those you are serving?

Anne Marie and Norman: Being involved with the poor and homeless makes one very sympathetic and compassionate to their difficulties in earning a living wage, finding affordable housing, and coping with the devastating impact of unemployment, illness, and addiction. The wave of immigration in the United States can be traced in those we've served over the years…initially our families were black (early 1970s); followed by Southeast Asians in the late 1970s and through the 1980s; also in the 1980s, Middle Easterners; then an explosion from Central and South America that continues today—all seeking a better life with very little resources; all being the face of Jesus to us.

Question: Has your joint service impacted your perception of the members of other churches with whom you're collaborating?

Anne Marie and Norman: We find that Protestant Churches and their members are often more dedicated to social justice issues than Catholic parishes. This is particularly true of the clergy. While there are many dedicated Catholic volunteers, there has always been reluctance on the part of the pastors of the three Catholic parishes in ACCA to lend their enthusiastic support, either financially or otherwise. There seems to be deep suspicion of any organization that is ecumenical, despite Vatican II's teachings on ecumenism. We would hope that with Pope Francis, our Catholic clergy would follow his dictum that "The shepherd should smell like his sheep."

Question: As you look back over time, how has your own faith life and spirituality been shaped and deepened by your involvement with ACCA?

Anne Marie and Norman: It has certainly made it clear that practicing one's religion is much more than church attendance on Sunday. It has allowed us to see how God works through people to do good and to have the opportunity to reach out in the love of Christ. In the words of Blessed Mother Teresa, it is in the "distressing disguise of the poor" that we see the face of God.

Question: Regarding the "witness of faith" dimension, what kind of things do you hear in the local civic community as to how ACCA's work is perceived by the public at large?

Anne Marie and Norman: The local community has a very high opinion of ACCA, particularly since we work largely with volunteers, spend little money on fundraising, and effectively address social issues. The financial support from the community, excluding grants from churches, is about a third of total revenues. We have never heard one word of criticism of what ACCA does, or how it does it. The high opinion of ACCA is also shared by such agencies as Fairfax County Social Services, United Way, the Combined Federal Campaign, and the Catalogue for Philanthropy.

Question: Would it be possible for you to share one experience that would give us a taste of your larger experience in this Christian Community for Action?

Anne Marie: Five years ago we met a Christian couple (ages forty and forty-three), pregnant with their first child, newly arrived refugees from Mosul, Iraq, where Christian persecution was rampant, speaking basically no English. The Holy Spirit put this couple in our path and the Spirit has guided us in clearing one hurdle after another. English classes were arranged; six months later their daughter, Miriam, was born (following a difficult pregnancy). The Holy Spirit arranged for an Arabic-speaking obstetrician to be on call, and I was blessed to be present at the birth. A Women's Choice (pro-life) Center provided a beautiful brand new crib and other baby needs, along with a baby shower. We are now Miriam's godparents.

Their housing at this time was substandard, with bed-bugs and no cooperation from the landlord. The county services had a ten-year waiting list for subsidized housing! With continued prayers to the Holy Spirit and pleas to the Arabic-speaking social worker, within two months they were granted a beautiful, clean, renovated, two-bedroom apartment in a safe neighborhood. Both Ibtisam and Saad are presently employed (low-paying jobs), but both are enrolled in community college classes to improve their situation. Both are now fluent in English, and Miriam is thriving and speaks perfect English. She will be in Kindergarten this fall. Five years ago, we could not communicate with words...today they are our dear friends far from the strife of Christian persecution in Mosul.

ACCA has been a God-sent support in these past five years with financial aid, food, transportation, etc., and has, for me, deepened my faith life. Miracles happened!

Question: Is there anything you would like to say to those who have never engaged in social action work like this and/or never done it with other Christians?

Anne Marie: We encourage all to reach out in love and service to those in need. It is a gentle reminder to be mindful of the blessings in our lives. Most of the time, one receives spiritually more than one gives.

Anne Marie's words apply to both individuals and communities. One of the principal means by which Christian communities give healthy witness is in their engagement in common mission at the service of those in need. The Canadian Catholic Bishops call such common mission the "dialogue of life" and observe that "we are nowhere near living out our common mission in the world to the extent that is appropriate and responsible."[22] The degree to which we share common faith convictions should translate into a corresponding degree of common mission in response to human need. Acting together on justice issues enhances our efforts; for when we speak with a united voice, we will have more impact than if we speak or stand alone. As ACCA exemplifies, there is vast and fertile ground here for practical collaboration in common mission.

7. ECUMENICAL FORMATION AND EDUCATION

It is not unusual for church historians to identify the ecumenical movement as a signal grace in the life of the church in the twentieth century. Does it strike you as surprising then to see how now, in the twenty-first century, there are a growing number of persons and groups in the churches who know little or nothing about the movement, its origins, aims, and vision? How many people still stumble even when trying to pronounce the word? Ecumenical apathy seems to be growing and concern about ecumenical ignorance is a long way down the list of preoccupations in most churches.

In the view of many, ecumenism was an optimistic twentieth-century attempt at unity that has been superseded by a retrenched denominationalism or by internal denominational strife or by post-denominationalism or by all three combined. While these perspectives do have some grounding in contemporary ecclesial realities, they cannot be the final word if we are to remain faithful to Jesus' call to and prayer for unity among his followers.[1]

WHAT IS ECUMENICAL FORMATION?

A study document, "Ecumenical Formation: Ecumenical Reflections and Suggestions" produced by the Joint Working Group between the World Council of Churches and the Roman Catholic Church offers this definition:

Ecumenical formation is an ongoing process of learning within the various local churches and world communions, aimed at informing and guiding people in the movement which—inspired by the Holy Spirit—seeks the visible unity of Christians.

This pilgrimage towards unity enables mutual sharing and mutual critique through which we grow. Such an approach to unity thus involves at once rootedness in Christ and in one's tradition, while endeavoring to discover and participate in the richness of other Christian and human traditions.[2]

While the language of formation and learning refer to some degree to a body of knowledge to be absorbed, formation and learning require a certain bold openness to *living* ecumenically as well. The 1952 Faith and Order conference in Lund, Sweden, made that point strongly early on in the process.

A faith in the one church of Christ which is not implemented by acts of obedience is dead. There are truths about the nature of God and his church which will remain for ever closed to us unless we act together in obedience to the unity which is already ours. We would, therefore, earnestly request our churches to consider whether they are doing all they ought to do to manifest the oneness of the people of God. Should not our churches ask themselves whether they are showing sufficient eagerness to enter into conversation with other churches and whether they would not act together in all matters except those in which deep differences of conviction compel them to act separately?...Obedience to God demands also that the churches seek unity in their mission to the world.[3]

The *Directory for the Application of Principles and Norms on Ecumenism* addresses the necessity and purpose of ecumenical formation in bold terms as well, underlining that it is not just for a few, but for *all*.

Concern for restoring unity pertains to the whole church, faithful and clergy alike. It extends to everyone, according to the potential of each, whether it be exercised in daily

Christian living or in theological and historical studies....For God's call to interior conversion and renewal in
the church, so fundamental to the quest for unity,
excludes no one. For that reason, all the faithful are called
upon to make a personal commitment toward promoting
increasing communion with other Christians.

The concern for unity is fundamental to the understanding of the church. The objective of ecumenical formation is that all Christians be animated by the
ecumenical spirit, whatever their particular mission and
task in the world and in society.[4]

These statements should make clear that "formation" is not to
be limited to programs of instruction and that it is more than training or even education. It refers to the whole process of equipping,
enabling, raising awareness, shaping or transforming attitudes and
values.[5]

In other words, the ecumenical movement is a learning movement, and that learning will take place across the whole of one's life
in a variety of ways: information, sharing of knowledge, dialogue
with people who belong to other traditions. Ecumenical learning will
be, then, integral to the formation of clergy and laity alike. While it
might occasionally take the form of particular programs, it is better
seen as a dimension of the whole educational task of the church. Its
emphasis is on *learning together with* rather than teaching, and it calls
us to transcend our limitations of culture, gender, and confession of
faith.[6]

Over the years, a number of specialized institutes for ecumenical study and research have been founded around the world. They
have a variety of purposes and go by a variety of names—study centers, dialogue centers, institutes for religion and culture, ecumenical
institutes—but all provide the context for a community of learning
that cuts across traditional divisions in the church.[7] A strongly motivating factor operative in the founding of each one of them is the
conviction that Christians must be helped to understand that to love
Jesus necessarily means to love everything Jesus prayed, lived, died,
and was raised for, namely "to gather into one the dispersed children

of God" (John 11:52) so that the unity of his disciples might be an effective sign of the unity of all peoples.[8]

The response to the prayer of Jesus "that they may all be one" (John 17:21) must be the response of everyone, said the Joint Working Group between the Roman Catholic Church and the World Council of Churches:

> Therefore, the growth into an ecumenical mind and heart is essential for each and for all, and the introduction of, and care for, ecumenical formation are absolutely necessary *at every level* of the church community, church life, action and activities; at *all* educational levels (schools, colleges, universities; theological schools, seminaries, religious/monastic communities, pastoral and lay formation centers; Sunday liturgies, homilies and catechesis).[9]

In short, ecumenical formation is a community process, not something intended for individuals only. Social and cultural factors must be taken into consideration. Among "suitable settings" for ecumenical formation, the Ecumenical Directory includes the family, the parish, the school, and different groups, associations, and ecclesial movements—"places where human and Christian maturity, the sense of companionship and communion, grow step by step."[10]

Different visions, profiles, and understandings of *ecumenical* have emerged over the decades. There is, on the one hand, an interpretation that places absolute priority on the efforts of fostering the unity of the church; on the other hand, there is the argument that Christian unity can never be an end in itself, but must be seen in the missionary perspective of serving as a sign and instrument for the unity of humankind. Then there is the emphasis on justice, peace, and the integrity of creation as embodying the ecumenical vision in its embrace of the whole inhabited earth (*oikoumene*). Furthermore, in the twenty-first century, there has been increasing reference to the notion of a "wider ecumenism," which goes beyond the Christian community in dialogue and collaboration with people of other faiths.[11]

All those perspectives should make it clear that the ecumenical movement is like a river with ever-new tributaries flowing through an ever-changing landscape, so it is not enough to put just one concern—whether unity, mission, or social responsibility—at the center. It will encompass them all at one time or another. Ecumenical formation will have to find ways of responding creatively to these tensions and diversities.

In that light, let us examine three different models for ecumenical formation—experiential, academic study, spirituality—and offer some reflections with regard to each approach.

EXPERIENTIAL

Let me share with you how I got involved in the ecumenical movement and how my faith and prayer have been shaped by it. During my theology studies in Washington, DC, our Paulist community provided rooms at our seminary residence for eight Lutheran students from their seminary in Gettysvania, Pennsylvania, who wanted to take some courses in Washington through its Theological Consortium. We, Catholic and Lutheran seminarians, lived on the same hallways, used the same library, shared study resources and meals together, enjoyed fellowship in the gathering space of the community room, and occasionally met for common prayer as well. We had the opportunity to experience ourselves as members of the one Body of Christ.

This experience influenced me to take a number of courses through the ecumenical Theological Consortium, courses sometimes offered in a different denominational seminary and taught by professors from other traditions of Christian faith. During one trimester involving intensive course work, I was offered the opportunity to go live at Episcopal Virginia Theological Seminary for a month where a scriptural course was being offered. Worshipping and studying the Bible together was often more educational than listening to lectures. This experience was further enriched by the concrete reality of living from morning to night over an extended period and in close proximity with ministry candidates in another tradition of our faith. The Ecumenical Directory recognizes that "in academic halls of residence there is very much to recommend good relations between Catholics and other Christian students. With suitable guidance, they can learn, through these relations, to live together in a deeper ecumenical spirit and be faithful witnesses of their Christian faith."[12]

My first assignment after ordination was in campus ministry at the Ohio State University in Columbus. The campus ministry association facilitated the various campus chaplains—Lutheran, Episcopal, Methodist, Baptist, Jewish—in working together in our pastoral outreach. Engaging in the ministry ecumenically felt very natural to me, given my lived experiences with Lutherans and Episcopalians during my years of seminary training.

I organized an evening dialogue series, inviting a group of students each week from a different denominational campus ministry center to come to the Newman Center and share with the Catholic students what they felt we should know about their tradition of Christian faith and what they loved about it. There was time for questions and answers to flow in both directions. I also initiated a marriage preparation program at the Newman Center that offered both plenary presentations and workshop options, and among the latter was a workshop for interchurch couples.

After three years at Ohio State, the Paulist community leadership was looking for someone to direct the Newman Centre at McGill University in Montreal. I saw the chance to exercise campus ministry in another cultural context as a valuable learning opportunity. In that McGill setting, the offices of some of the various ministers on campus were all located in the same building, a large house across the street from the campus, where we met regularly to discuss how we might be more effective.

In the meantime, the Catholic archbishop, noting my ecumenical interest, invited me to represent the English-speaking Catholic community on the Montreal Council of Churches. His representative for the French-speaking constituency was the founder-director of the Canadian Centre for Ecumenism, Fr. Irenée Beaubien, SJ. We became friends over the next couple years, and one day he came to visit me at the Newman Center and offered me the position of associate director that had just come open at the national Montreal-based ecumenical center that he directed. After receiving enthusiastic support from our Paulist leadership, I entered into a year-long process of intensive ecumenical formation to prepare for ministry at the national and international level.

Fr. Beaubien encouraged me to set up the kind of experience that would most effectively facilitate my learning. As I have always learned best by being put in the situation, letting the questions arise, and then proceeding with dialogue and study, I fashioned a year that would integrate the experiential with academic study.

I began with the Canterbury Ecumenical Summer School in England. It was essentially an international Anglican gathering, but the twenty or so of us who were in the Presbyterian, United Reformed, Baptist, Lutheran, United Church, Roman Catholic, and Disciples of Christ traditions were warmly welcomed. Under the theme of "The Servants of God," we studied the teachings and exam-ple of St. Augustine, St. Francis, St. Anselm, Martin Luther, John Wesley, Cardinal Newman, Karl Barth, and Teilhard de Chardin. We shared morning and evening prayer, sometimes in the sacred air of Canterbury Cathedral, and visited many of the revered historic sites.

From England I went to Switzerland for a four-month graduate school semester at the Ecumenical Institute of Bossey, the World Council of Churches's study center about twelve miles outside of Geneva, overlooking the lake and facing the French Alps. In our class were fifty-five people, lay and clergy, from thirty-five different countries and twenty-one different denominations. Being the only Roman Catholic in the group, I knew my opportunities for learning would be greater than most and not always comfortable.

Why had we come? The goals of the graduate school, affiliated with the University of Geneva, told the story: to provide training for future generations of ecumenical leaders; to promote ecumenical theology within the context of intercultural and interconfessional encounters; to share in an ecumenical spirituality that respects the diversity of liturgical traditions; to create a community in which ecu-menism is *experienced* and shared.

In temporary residential learning contexts such as this, every-one starts out feeling like a stranger, but the initial feeling of estrangement becomes an excellent means for rediscovering the pil-grim nature of the Christian life, and a feeling of fellowship is grad-ually created. Experiencing vulnerability and discomfort for a time can foreshadow real growth. Studying, worshipping, living together creates deep levels of personal involvement. Experiences outside the classroom are just as important as those inside the classroom.

Within a divided world and divided churches, it is a joy to be able to pray together daily as Christians from different confessions and cultures. That said, the chapel is also a place of discomfort as differences in spirituality and liturgical traditions are strongly felt and a common Eucharist is still not possible. Nevertheless, as the community grows, a common heritage in prayers and hymns is also discovered and new forms of common celebrations are developed. For many Protestants, the exposure to Roman Catholic and Orthodox practices is central to their experiences of growth and increased openness, and vice versa.

In an era of globalization, Bossey offers unique opportunities for ecumenical formation in an interconfessional, intercultural, and international community. It offers an opportunity for Christian people, both lay and clergy, to come to terms with diversity and plurality. It is a laboratory not only for interconfessional encounter and dialogue, but for intercultural living.[13]

Not surprisingly, a number of Bossey graduates have subsequently become ecumenical officers in their own communions and have been instrumental in fostering their communion's general ecumenical involvement. Participation in multilayered experiential education such as this helps one develop significant skills for coping with diversity, conflict, ambiguity, and change—the very traits characterizing the increasingly pluralistic and multicultural environment in North America. Our current educational trends of distant and online learning can lead away from intentional community as a preparation for ministry and pastoral leadership. There is no substitute for up close interpersonal connection. In our current cultural context, there is a crisis of values, identity, and the ability to live a faithful life in communities of people with diverse backgrounds, interests, and needs. Such a context makes ecumenical formation both more challenging and more important than ever because it addresses the essence of real Christian unity.[14]

After the Bossey Graduate School, I turned to the East for an immersion experience with the Coptic Orthodox, one of the six Oriental Orthodox Churches,[15] visiting several of their churches in Cairo, Egypt, before sojourning in the desert monastery of St. Macarius between Cairo and Alexandria. From there, I went to Jerusalem to live successive Western and Eastern Holy Weeks, before going on to Mount Athos, a peninsula in northern Greece, to spend some days in several Eastern Orthodox monasteries. Exploration and integration are more than schooling. They come through the experience of a journey with others outside our group or tribe or clan. We learn from the experience of living together, speaking together, and being together.

The learnings and blessings from that year of concentrated ecumenical formation were indeed a gift, one that was not meant to be kept for myself but to be shared with others. One of the forms that desire took was the book *Tales of Christian Unity: The Adventures of an Ecumenical Pilgrim.*[16] The opportunity to live such extraordinary experiences was exceptional, and such an overview makes the nature of experiential learning clear.

When I returned to Montreal, it was time to put the fruits of those formative experiences at the service of the church at-large, and did so over the next fourteen years at the Canadian Centre for Ecumenism (CCE), serving for the last eleven as its director. The work was rich and varied: editing the Centre's international quarterly journal; participating in national interchurch dialogues; initiating five-day summer ecumenical institutes in different provinces; preaching ecumenical parish missions with an Anglican preaching partner; participating in provincial, national, and international ecumenical networks; and yes, writing another book that shared the journey and learning of those years: *A Survival Guide for Ecumenically Minded Christians.*[17]

And when I left the CCE, it was to lead the way in founding an ecumenical center for spirituality and Christian meditation, *Unitas* (in Latin, "unity"), which was cosponsored by eight different denominations and provided one of those much-needed places where Christians can gather and strengthen one another in the faith through shared life and prayer. After serving as its director for five years, the Paulist community leadership called me to open, develop, and direct the work of a North American office that would give expression to our community's commitment to the work for Christian unity and interreligious relations.

Overall, the ministry has not only been forged by but continues to be marked by an experiential character in events such as retreats that bring people from different traditions together; ecumenical parish missions with a Protestant preaching partner that bring whole congregations together; and ecumenical and interreligious study tours.

ACADEMIC STUDY AND LEARNING

The necessity of formation in order to fulfill God's mission is obvious. At a moment of history when churches and Christians have become aware that unity is a fundamental condition of faithfulness to God's missionary commandment, such formation has to be strongly influenced by an ecumenical orientation. If theological education does not hold this as a clear value, and if the quest for Christian unity, common witness, and service is not addressed in intentionally defined courses of study, the ecumenical memory and vision of the future will be lost.[18]

SEMINARIES

The training and preparation of leaders in the ecumenical movement cannot be left to chance. The movement needs a new generation of ecumenical practitioners who are aware of the breakthroughs of the past and who have a fire in their hearts to carry those advances forward into the future and build upon them.

An education, for example, that relates to the fruits of the bilateral and multilateral dialogues can help people overcome misinformed or outdated prejudices against other Christian traditions. Clergy would then be more prepared to preach and teach about the riches in other churches and ecclesial communities and to invite parishioners to visit and learn from them. Several of the bilateral dialogues have expressed the hope that their ecumenical work would make a difference in theological education. The Lutheran-Roman Catholic Dialogue, in its report "Ways to Community," states, "Since both the success and failure of ecumenical rapprochement depend heavily on the church's ministers, stress must be laid on their acquiring *ecumenical awareness and experience*. Ecumenical awareness needs to be developed by permeating *theological education* with ecumenism."[19] An Anglican-Methodist dialogue document, "Sharing in the Apostolic Communion," proposed that "joint courses might be offered in theological schools" as a way of drawing the two communions closer to each other.[20]

Dr. Mitzi Budde, a Lutheran who teaches elective courses in ecumenism at the Virginia Episcopal Seminary and is currently president of the North American Academy of Ecumenists, reflects on her experience:

Seminaries conscientiously teach students the history of the church's divisions: early church heresies, Reformation disputes, modern denominationalism. Yet we also need to teach the quest for unity. When I teach students, usually I find them well educated about these theological divisions, but *not* about the decades of ecumenical dialogue that have addressed and, in many cases, bridged these divisions. We re-inculcate the divisions of the church into every successive generation.

Transmitting an ecumenical spirit to the next generation will involve training clergy for ecumenical reception in the local church, developing church leaders who are knowledgeable of past ecumenical dialogues and prepared to continue the work for the future, nurturing those who wish to prepare for calls in full-communion partner churches, and inculcating an ecumenical spirit in all church leaders.[21]

Newly ordained ministers and future congregational leaders will soon find themselves in their parish work dealing with ecumenical situations like premarital counseling for and celebration of interchurch marriages; baptism and first communion in interchurch families; recommendations around forms of shared prayer in the home; joint educational opportunities in vacation bible schools and summer youth camps; and shared service opportunities like shelters and food pantries in the local area.[22]

Dr. Budde underscores why seminary communities and denominational leaders need to pay particular attention to fostering ecumenical vision and vocation in seminary education:

Church leaders in the twenty-first century face a complex web of contexts for ministry, many of them inherently ecumenical. Students of all denominations need to be equipped to serve in a religious world that is, paradoxically, both more interconnected and more fragmented than ever before. The changing context of the Church, the seminaries, the ecumenical movement and the world demands of clergy and lay leaders a solid foundation for the ecumenical aspects of ministry.

The congregations that American seminarians will serve in the twenty-first century are no longer homogenous groups of folk raised in that denominational tradition. The average American local parish is an ecumenical experience within its own four walls. Many congregations now include significant numbers of people on a personal ecumenical journey. Many have changed denominations, for various reasons: a mid-life faith awakening, a tragedy that brings soul-searching, a desire for a change in the routine of faith life, a moral conflict with a denomination's chosen ethical stance, a theological dispute, or simply geographic convenience. The number of ecumenical marriages has increased dramatically, and frequently the marriage partners from another tradition attend worship in their spouse's church, though often they do not join.

Some laity lack a strong commitment to a theological tradition and are "church shopping"....What may look on the surface to be "church shopping" may actually be a layperson's search for a parish with preaching, liturgy, and hymnody that fit his/her own worldview. The old barriers of family church affiliation, loyalty to a denominational tradition, or interpretation of one's tradition as the only "true" church have, for the most part, broken down in American church society.

How are seminary graduates prepared to deal with this new phenomenon? Successful parish clergy are able to speak to these ecumenical laity intelligently, respectfully, and in theologically articulate ways. Ecumenism at the local level in the twenty-first century is no longer primarily the relationship with the parish down the street (as important as that may continue to be). Rather the new ecumenism begins within the walls and pews of each congregation. An informed knowledge of other denominations and of the ecumenical movement is now an essential part of effective church ministry.[23]

I interviewed Dr. Larry Golemon, Director of the Washington Theological Consortium, a community of theological schools of diverse Christian traditions with partners in education, spirituality, and interfaith dialogue, regarding his perceptions of ecumenical formation. He shared that, while several seminaries include ecumenical and interfaith education as part of the degree goals for Masters programs, it is difficult to find explicit core courses dedicated to either. At best, an "academic area" requirement asks students to take a course with an ecumenical or interfaith dimension, which often entails registering for a course in another Consortium school. However, that course can be in any field of the curriculum, like Bible study or history, and not have an ecumenical or interreligious focus.

Dr. Golemon also pointed out that most of the seminaries in the Consortium do have core courses involving Catholic, Protestant, and Eastern Orthodox theologians who utilize ecumenical texts and topics in the broad sense. For example, the biblical courses utilize modern commentaries and authors that are almost always from various traditions. And certain fields of study such as mission, evangelism, and ecclesiology involve resources and interlocutors from various Christian traditions. Therefore, one could say that the church's mission for unity is happening organically. However, while these courses are inherently interdenominational in one sense, Christian unity, as such, is not their primary goal or vision.

The Ecumenical Directory, for its part, is clearly looking for more when it states,

> Even though an ecumenical dimension should permeate all theological formation, it is of particular importance that a course in ecumenism be given at an appropriate point in the first cycle. Such a course should be compulsory.
>
> It would be good if a general introduction to ecumenism were offered fairly early so that the students could be sensitized, right from the beginning of their theological studies, to the ecumenical dimension of their studies. This introduction would deal with the basic questions in ecumenism.
>
> In the second cycle, too, ecumenical questions should be carefully treated, as directed by competent ecclesiastical authority. In other words, it will be opportune to give courses of specialization in ecumenism.
>
> Doctrinal formation and learning experience are not

limited to the period of formation, but ask for a continu-
ous *aggiornamento* of the ordained ministers and pastoral
workers, in view of the continual evolution within the
ecumenical movement.[24]

Two years after the Ecumenical Directory was issued, the
Pontifical Council for Promoting Christian Unity published the
study document, "The Ecumenical Dimension in the Formation of
Those Engaged in Pastoral Work," offering a more detailed description of the ecumenical formation desired.[25]

The Joint Working Group between the Vatican and the World
Council of Churches, for its part, reflected that "Ecumenical formation is meant to help set the tone and perspective of every instruction and, therefore, may demand a change in the orientation of our
educational institutions, systems and curricula."[26]

Education courses should also have an experiential component
and not be limited to reading books, articles, and dialogue documents, and writing papers. This might take the form of shared worship, inviting preachers from other traditions to occasionally break
open the word of God at one's own school or chapel, and inviting in
representatives of other denominations to teach devotional practices
for which they have high regard in their own tradition and to
respond to any questions about them.

Furthermore, ecumenical formation can no longer be limited to
nurturing a sense of unity among the different Christian traditions,
but should aim as well at equipping and enabling Christian people to
respond creatively to the situation in our society today of growing
religious diversity with people of different world religions living and
working side by side.

ECUMENICAL FORMATION PROGRAMS
FOR CLERGY AND LAITY

Unfortunately, ecumenical formation programs are few and far
between. In addition to the four-month program at the Ecumenical
Institute of Bossey[27] in Switzerland that I described above, here are
four others.

Centro Pro Unione in Rome: The Franciscan Friars of the
Atonement have been offering a three-week summer program at the

Centro Pro Unione in Rome since 1992.[28] This course is designed to introduce participants to the ecumenical and interreligious movements from a Catholic perspective. It offers a historical and theological overview of the issues that divide Christians as well as the bonds that unite them. The program also explores relations with other world religions. The course, which is in English, is for men and women who are in preparation for ministry or religious life, who are in the mission field, who are ecumenical officers or members of ecumenical commissions, or who are looking for a sabbatical experience led by qualified professors and ecumenists.

Monday through Friday, the morning begins with prayer, followed by three sixty-minute lectures. The afternoons are for onsite excursions and lectures at places such as the Roman catacombs; the Basilica of St. Peter and excavations; the "Roman ghetto"; the synagogue and museum; and the Islamic center and mosque.

The first week focuses on "The Reformation, both Protestant and Catholic," with an eye to biblical foundations; factions and divisions within the church; an overview of the Reformation and Catholic Reform movements; the modern ecumenical movement; the Second Vatican Council and the principles of Catholic ecumenism; World Council of Churches; worldwide ecumenical and interreligious organizations; and Eastern Christianity.

The second week's theme is "From Division to Dialogue" and involves an exploration of the various dialogues that exist between the churches, their context and results; ecumenical documents; reading of ecumenical texts; the concept of reception in the ecumenical movement; and includes a visit to the Pontifical Councils for Promoting Christian Unity and for Interreligious Dialogue.

In the third week, the field of study broadens to "Christians and World Faith Traditions" with attention to Jewish-Christian relations; Christian responses to people of other faiths; fundamentalism as a worldwide phenomenon; Catholicism and Islam in dialogue; new religious movements; and grassroots ecumenism.

The Director of the Centro Pro Unione is the Rev. Fr. James Puglisi, SA, PhD, professor of Ecumenical Theology at the Pontifical University of St. Thomas (the Angelicum) in Rome. The faculty includes, but is not limited to, staff members of the Centro Pro Unione and the Graymoor Ecumenical and Interreligious Institute in

New York. The course is recognized and endorsed by the Graduate Theological Foundation (USA),[29] which can grant up to six graduate credits for qualified graduate students.

The Catholic Association of Diocesan Ecumenical and Interreligious Officers (CADEIO): CADEIO offers an annual Introductory Ecumenical Leadership Institute that is open to new ecumenical and interreligious officers, commission members, diocesan leaders, members of religious orders, seminarians, theology students, and interested laity. It presently runs from a Monday evening to Thursday afternoon, and provides a foundation in related church documents, an overview of relationships with ecumenical partners, and attention to the dynamics of dialogue. Every other year, CADEIO also offers the Advanced Institute for Ecumenical Leadership, which offers a week-long deeper study of the dialogues and their progress, a closer look at the Eastern Churches, and a sharing of concerns relating to current issues. The location of these programs can vary from year to year.[30]

The Institute for Ecumenical Research: Located in Strasbourg, France, the institute, on behalf of the world's Lutheran churches, brings together under one roof a multinational team of theologians providing theological analysis and advice, serving the churches as they strive to resolve their differences and thus make visible the unity of the Church under one Lord, Jesus Christ. Established in 1965, the Institute carries out its work by theological research in areas where Christian churches are divided in matters of doctrine and church order. It offers an annual eight-day theological Summer Seminar to share the findings and breakthroughs of the ecumenical movement with a wider audience. Over the course of almost five decades, the Summer Seminars have explored a rich range of subjects, from Mary, liturgy, and the sacraments to ethics, church-state relations, and mission. Participants from Europe and farther abroad gather for a week of lectures offered by specialists in their fields, as well as daily prayer and shared meals.[31]

Program in Ecumenical Studies and Formation: This new program was launched in 2014 by the Prairie Centre for Ecumenism in Saskatoon, Saskatchewan.[32] It is a three-year program, dedicated to forming Christians in the theology, history, and practice of ecumenism within the churches of Canada and abroad. The intended audience of this program includes ecumenical officers; people in training for ministry; ministry practitioners whose work is located within an ecumenical setting; and laypeople who wish to increase their knowledge of the ecumenical movement for greater participation. The program assumes no prior theological training and is offered in the final week of June each summer.

The first-year program consists of seven modules containing the following units: "Biblical Foundations of Ecumenism"; "Spiritual Ecumenism"; "The History of Ecumenism"; and two modules on "The Principles of Ecumenical Theology." Along with these units, participants share an introductory session dedicated to "Mapping Ecumenism" and an integration session at the completion of their time together. Participants then complete their first year of studies with an eighth and final unit of self-directed study at home in their local ecumenical context. In each succeeding year, the first-year curriculum is offered simultaneously with one of the two groupings of advanced modules.

The second and third years of the program are comprised of a series of advanced modules dedicated to the following themes: ecumenical dialogues (theory, attitudes, methods, as well as discussion of actual dialogues); the practice of ecumenism in common witness and mission; ecumenical covenants; ecumenism and interreligious dialogue; cultural issues in ecumenical dialogue and common ministry; the practice of ecumenical courtesy; ecumenical leadership; interchurch families; challenging issues such as eucharistic sharing, sexuality and gender, papacy and Petrine ministry; ecumenism and social justice; and religious freedom. There is also a study component with assigned reading and a writing assignment after each year's program.

The whole cycle of study is aimed at deepening understanding and commitment to the call to Christian reconciliation and unity. "There really is no other program like it active anywhere in North America," says Dr. Darren Dahl, director of the Prairie Centre for Ecumenism.[33] Upon completing the three-year cycle, participants will receive a certificate from St. Andrew's College, a theological college operated by the United Church of Canada on the University of Saskatchewan campus.

The program, which includes prayer and worship, seeks to bring together laity and clergy from all the Christian churches. The first-year class included participants with a range of backgrounds and representing a variety of Christian denominations. Saskatoon Roman Catholic Bishop Donald Bolen, who served for seven years on the Pontifical Council for Promoting Christian Unity in Rome with responsibility for relations with Anglicans and the World Methodist Council, is enthusiastic about the initiative: "With the launch of this program, the Prairie Centre is taking a major step toward the formation of ecumenical leaders for the future, not just for our region, but potentially for participants from far and wide, given the lack of such programs elsewhere and their urgent need."[34]

LAY COLLABORATORS, PARISHES, AND SCHOOLS

The Pontifical Council for Promoting Christian Unity's document "The Ecumenical Dimension in the Formation of Those Engaged in Pastoral Work" highlights "the necessity of ecumenical formation for all Christ's faithful"—families and schools, parishes and organizations—so that every Christian might make their particular contributions to Christian unity (1–2). Such formation is to cultivate a knowledge of Catholic ecumenical principles and how they apply to a wide range of pastoral situations; to provide an acquaintance with ecumenical organizations and structures; to foster an awareness of the results of ecumenical dialogues; and to convey an understanding of both common ground and remaining disagreements (16). Where appropriate, teachers from other Christian communities are to be called upon "to present their ecclesial traditions of Christian faith and ways of living it out" (10). This formation should foster "an authentically ecumenical disposition," "enliven ecumenical *conversion* and *commitment*," and be accompanied by practical ecumenical experience (9).[35]

An essential starting point is getting to know other Christians and Christian communities. This happens through friendship, praying, and acting together in mission and witness. Adult faith formation can include bringing Christians of different traditions together to deepen their knowledge of the faith and of one another.[36]

For its part, the Ecumenical Directory says that the formation and education norms for the theological institutes also apply to the study programs for other recognized collaborators in pastoral work—catechists, teachers, and other lay helpers—recognizing the need for adaptation to the level of these participants and their studies.[37] It also notes that theology faculties and institutes of higher learning as well as seminaries and other institutes of formation can contribute to ongoing formation for church workers either by arranging courses for those involved in pastoral work or by providing teachers or subsidies for workshops and courses offered by others.[38]

The Ecumenical Directory calls for "systematic instruction of priests, religious, deacons and laity on the present state of the ecumenical movement so that they may be able to introduce the ecumenical viewpoint into preaching, catechesis, prayer, and Christian life in general."[39] In other words, parishes are to be a place of authentic ecumenical witness and to educate their members in the ecumenical spirit. It recommends that each parish designate someone who will be charged with planning and promoting ecumenical activity, working in close harmony with the parish priest to help in the various forms of collaboration with neighboring congregations of other Christians.[40]

The school, too—"of every kind and grade"—has an important role to play. It should give an ecumenical dimension to its religious teaching, aiming in its own way to train hearts and minds in human and religious values, educating for dialogue, peace, and personal relationships, for "the spirit of charity, of respect and dialogue demands the elimination of language and prejudices which distort the image of other Christians….The young must grow in faith, in prayer, in resolve to put into practice the Christian Gospel of unity."[41]

An even more important role is given to the family, the domestic church, as the primary place in which unity will be fashioned or weakened each day. Awareness of its Christian identity and mission will make the family ready to be a community for others, a community ready for dialogue and social involvement. The Ecumenical Directory has a special word for interchurch families who "have the duty to proclaim Christ with the fullness implied in a common baptism" and who "have, too, the delicate task of making themselves builders of unity."[42]

Other initiatives encouraged by the Ecumenical Directory are collaboration in social and charitable initiatives in contexts such as schools, hospitals, and prisons, as well as work for peace, human rights, and religious liberty.

When the church focuses on the needs of the local community and of the world, on its pain and suffering, denominationalism becomes relativized and ecumenical commitment is strengthened. Ecumenical engagement provides a renewing vision marked by four identifiable features:

a *holistic* vision: beyond dualisms of gender, body-soul or body-mind, spiritual-natural, visible-invisible;

a *healing* vision: transforming the human, social, and ecological condition;

a *communal* vision: emphasizing and celebrating the human family tree of interrelatedness and partnership; and

an *ecumenical* vision: inclusive of all denominations and of people of other faiths, recognizing all God's children in God's image.[43]

THE DEVELOPMENT OF AN ECUMENICAL SPIRITUALITY

In his high priestly prayer, Jesus prayed for all those who will believe in him, "that they may all be one. As you, Father, are in me and I am in you, may they also be in us, so that the world may believe that you have sent me. The glory that you have given me I have given them, so that they may be one, as we are one" (John 17:21–22).

This is the ecumenical imperative. It is Christ's will for us that we manifest before the world the unity we have been given in Christ so that the world may believe. It is a unity that is grounded in and reflects the communion that exists between the Father and the Son and the Holy Spirit. Evangelization and ecumenism are two sides of one coin; the ecumenical imperative and the mission of the church are inextricably intertwined for the salvation of all.[44] The goal of the ecumenical movement is the unity of the church for the sake of the unity of humankind. That is the vision that should shape our processes of formation.

Doctrine and theology without spirituality are empty. It follows from the ecumenical imperative that the process of formation in ecumenism has to be undergirded by, and should be an expression of, ecumenical spirituality. It is spiritual in that it should be open to the prayer of Jesus for unity and to the promptings of the Holy Spirit who reconciles us. It is also spiritual in that it leads us to repentance for our past disobedience that has been marked by contentiousness and hostility at every level. And it is spiritual in the sense of seeking a renewed lifestyle that is characterized by sacrificial love, compassion, patience with one another, and tolerance.[45]

Clearly, the church's mission requires patience and perseverance in order to complete the mosaic vision of unity that the Spirit is creating over space and time. This takes spiritual depth and requires the disciplines of regular prayer and meditation on Scripture. Without a mature spiritual life, we soon fall by the wayside and lose hope. It requires a deep faith and trust that God, in God's own wisdom and timing, will bless us with this gift of giving more visible expression to our unity in diversity.

Dr. Philip Potter, who served several years as general secretary of the World Council of Churches, argued that the distinctive feature of ecumenical research and study must be the spirituality of unity. For it is God's grace, self-giving love, and commitment to us and to all human beings that makes us what we are and enables us to work for the unity of the church. Recognizing that this grace is shared in different ways with different persons, our task is to build up the Body of Christ into the unity of faith. The study and research involved should be characterized by three things. First, freedom, in faithfulness to the movement of the Holy Spirit, for "where the Spirit of the Lord is, there is freedom" (2 Cor 3:17). Second, it will be anchored in the word of God. Third, it will be undertaken in the mood of prayer and worship, as a search to receive illumination from God and as an act of celebration.[46]

In the ecumenical movement, it is necessary to give priority to conversion of heart, spiritual life and its renewal. As Vatican II's Decree on Ecumenism put it, "This change of heart and holiness of life, along with public and private prayer for the unity of Christians, should be regarded as the soul of the whole ecumenical movement and can rightly be called *spiritual ecumenism*" (no. 8).

One of the forms that spiritual ecumenism takes is giving value to sources of spiritual life that are found in other churches and that belong to the one church of Christ: Holy Scripture, the sacraments, and other sacred actions or devotions that cultivate faith, hope, charity, and other gifts of the Holy Spirit. The Ecumenical Directory notes that these goods are manifest in the mystical tradition of the Christian East and the spiritual treasures of the monastic life; in the worship and piety of Anglicans; and in the evangelical prayer and the diverse forms of Protestant spirituality. The appreciation of these gifts should not remain merely theoretical, but be marked by the practical knowledge of other traditions of spirituality and find expression in shared prayer and other devotional acts in accord with existing directives.[47]

My own year of ecumenical formation was a "year of blessing." I brought back practices from my experience of shared life, prayer, and worship that took root and grew in my own spiritual life and have been a source of immense enrichment: the Jesus Prayer of the Christian East; the veneration of icons; the psalms as a prayer of the universal church; an increased appreciation for singing the faith; daily reading and reflection on the scriptures; the depth and richness of the Christian tradition of contemplative prayer.

Emphasis should be given to prayer for unity, not only during the annual Week of Prayer, but also at other times during the year. Ecumenical worship provides an experiential component. It is through particular prayer forms that we communicate our living spirituality to one another. It is common for ecumenical communities such as Taizé in Southern France, Grandchamp in Switzerland, Bose in Italy, Corymeela in Northern Ireland, and Iona in Scotland to develop patterns of worship that draw on the resources of spirituality of the different Christian traditions and cultures. And it is not uncommon that people's hearts are deeply touched and their minds opened through their experience in worship.

Other forms that shared prayer might take are joint retreats, or sharing cherished spiritual texts and hymns with one another in the hope that such familiarity will contribute to effecting change of heart and attitudes toward each other, which itself is a gift of the Holy Spirit. Such efforts will help us live constructively and with awareness of the reality and pain of division, while deepening mutual trust and making it possible to open our hearts to the positive aspects of one another's traditions. Prayer for unity creates a hunger for unity.[48]

In other words, we need to cultivate an appreciation for the catholicity of the church, which encompasses such a wondrous variety of cultures and histories, and for the diversity of gifts that God has given churches to hold in trust for the whole body. Dr. Golemon said that he finds courses in spirituality are some of the most effective means in creating a "gift exchange" between Christian traditions, as Catholics and Protestants often learn of spiritual disciplines and devotional practices from which their own traditions can grow. The transdenominational migrations of the Ignatian spiritual exercises or Protestant hymnody testify to the hunger for sharing and appropriating such gifts. He also felt that some of the most effective formation experiences happen through immersion courses or study tours such as trips to Canterbury, Rome, or Istanbul. My own early and recent experiences confirm that, as a few years ago I co-led a Unity and Reconciliation Study Tour to Northern Ireland; central England; Switzerland; and Taizé in France. In each place, we drew inspiration from people in various centers and communities who are devoting themselves to healing the wounds of division in the Body of Christ.

The conviction that ecumenism is not an option for the churches but a gospel imperative is fundamental. The document, "Ecumenical Formation," by the Joint Working Group between the Roman Catholic Church and the World Council of Churches puts it this way:

> Ecumenism is not an option for the churches. In obedience to Christ and for the sake of the world the churches are called to be an effective sign of God's presence and compassion before all the nations. For the churches to come divided to a broken world is to undermine their credibility when they claim to have a ministry of universal unity and reconciliation. The ecumenical imperative must be heard and responded to everywhere. This response necessarily requires ecumenical formation which will help the people of God to render a common witness to all humankind by pointing to the vision of the new heaven and a new earth (Rev 21:1).[49]

8. SPIRITUAL AND RECEPTIVE ECUMENISM

In the last fifty years, the movement for unity among Christians has made significant gains through the international and national dialogues that have led to considerable *rapprochement* and in some cases to consensus. Despite this positive progress, however, the dialogues are finding it challenging to maintain positive momentum in the face of newly surfacing questions emerging from the culture wars of our times. One of the present challenges is to keep air in the tires of the important work of doctrinal reconciliation and the effort to set up collaborative and uniting structures between different Christian communions. The danger is that the ecumenical movement can become so preoccupied with conferences, committees, dialogues, and reports that it can just come to feel like office work rather than something Spirit-led. Whenever ecumenism "moves," it is not our achievement we celebrate, but God's, for God is the chief actor in this movement. And since God is the center, the closer we draw to God, the closer we draw to one another. The positive side of no longer being able to revel in institutional success may well be that it brings us back to this revitalizing realization.[1] Toward that end, an impetus is needed that is greater and stronger than the academic conversations and committee background work can be by their nature. In this critical situation, we have to return to the original and basic impetus of the ecumenical movement.[2]

From its very inception, the ecumenical movement was rooted in the soil of spiritual inspiration. In 1907, Fr. Paul Wattson, the founder of the Society of the Atonement, a Franciscan religious community within the Episcopal Church that later joined the Catholic

Church in New York, offered the idea of an octave (eight days) of prayer between the feasts of St. Peter's Chair on January 18 and that of the Conversion of St. Paul on January 25. A year later it was initiated. In 1935, Abbé Paul Couturier, a priest of the archdiocese of Lyons in France, gave the Week of Prayer new energy by reframing it and bringing more Protestants into the circle. The prayer proposed by Wattson was for the return of other Christians to the unity of the Catholic Church. Couturier took another approach: that all Christians pray together that they might be more fully converted to Christ and to the unity Christ desires for them. He called for them to pray for unity "as Christ wills it and when he wills it," and he named such prayer "spiritual ecumenism." Couturier's more Christ-centered approach evoked a spirituality of conversion for all the churches so that each and all together might become more fully church.

Vatican II's Decree on Ecumenism picked up on the theme saying that "There can be no ecumenism worthy of the name without interior conversion....This change of heart and holiness of life, along with public and private prayer for the unity of Christians, should be regarded as the soul of the whole ecumenical movement, and merits the name, 'spiritual ecumenism'" (nos. 7, 8).

Spiritual ecumenism is seen as an opening of ourselves to the transformational power of the Holy Spirit, who changes our hearts and leads us to repentance, conversion, and holiness of life. And in this completely spiritual space, we place ourselves before God and ask whether we have been faithful to God's plan for the church. This humble attitude of heart is the necessary ground and environment enabling the quest for Christian unity to be both fruitful and sustained.

Repentance and conversion are called for because, as the Decree said in its opening lines, our division "openly contradicts the will of Christ, scandalizes the world, and damages that most holy cause, the preaching of the Gospel to every creature" (no. 1). To confront this scandal and to work to overcome it presupposes a profound spirituality. We will only make progress in our work for Christian unity when we engage in returning to its spiritual roots. If we relate to the source of that original impetus as though it were simply our starting point that we have now left behind us, rather than one that must always accompany us, we will find it necessary to pull off the road because our tires are flat. As Cardinal Walter Kasper wrote while head of the Pontifical Council for Promoting Christian Unity:

> We will only be able to make progress if we return to our spiritual roots and search for a renewed ecumenical spirituality. That means listening and opening ourselves to the demands of the Spirit who speaks through various forms of piety. A spiritual empathy is needed, an intimate understanding from the inside, with the heart as well as with the mind, of what may be for us initially strange Christian and ecclesial forms of life. Spiritual ecumenism involves a readiness to rethink, to bear the otherness of the other. It requires tolerance, patience, respect, good will and love which does not boast but rejoices in the truth (1 Cor 13:4–6).[3]

This induction into an ever greater and deeper truth is the work of the Holy Spirit who leads us into the whole truth. The Spirit does this in a variety of ways, one of which is spiritual experience. Ecumenical dialogue is not only an exchange of ideas, but an exchange of spiritual gifts and experiences. When we move closer to Jesus Christ through the exchange of our different denominational experiences, we gradually grow into full stature in him. He is our unity. As Kasper notes, in him we can historically realize the wholeness and fullness of catholicity after overcoming our divisions.

> The unity of the church cannot be some abstract system that, in a lucky hour, was discovered and agreed upon in a theological dialogue. There is no doubt that theological agreement is necessary. But in the end unity can only be understood and accepted in a spiritual experience that, naturally, cannot only be an individual one but must have ecclesial character. It is an act of trust in the fact that the other, with the different forms and formulas, the different pictures, symbols and concepts, means and believes the same mystery of faith that we retain in our traditions. According to theological teaching, such a consensus is the work and sign of the Holy Spirit (*Lumen Gentium*, 12)....It is not up to us to set deadlines; the Spirit alone

determines the time. Ecumenism was from the beginning a spiritual phenomenon. Where ecumenical consensus has been possible, it has always been experienced as a spiritual gift.[4]

If we are to walk forward on strong legs with our heads up in the ecumenical journey, avoiding resignation, it will be through our reliance on the Holy Spirit who will show us the way and give us more than we dare to hope or dream.

SPIRITUAL ECUMENISM IN PRACTICE

At the top of the list of marks of spiritual ecumenism is prayer for unity. "The measure of our concern for unity," said the delegates to the World Council of Churches' Second Assembly in 1954, "is the degree to which we pray for it. We cannot expect God to give us the unity unless we prepare ourselves to receive his gift by costly and purifying prayer. To pray together is to be drawn together."[5] John Paul II told the College of Cardinals in a state-of-the-Catholic Church address: "I pray every day for Christian unity." I wonder how many Christians could say as much. Imagine what a different church it would be if many members in all the churches that make up the one church of Christ could say the same.

It would make a difference because prayer's first effect is in us. Our own hearts and minds would be shaped by our own prayer and become more sensitive to the opportunities we have to translate that prayer into practice. Prayer is and will always hold the first place in unity efforts because it is prayer that most changes our hearts, and it is our hearts that most need to be changed.[6]

At the 20th World Youth Day in 2005, Pope Benedict XVI said, "We can only obtain unity as a gift of the Holy Spirit. Consequently, spiritual ecumenism—prayer, conversion and the sanctification of life—constitutes the heart of the…ecumenical movement....I am convinced that if more and more people unite themselves interiorly to the Lord's prayer 'that all may be one' (John 17:21), then this prayer, made in the Name of Jesus, will not go unheard (cf. John 14:13; 15:7, 16, etc.)."[7]

Similarly, in a general audience in St. Peter's Square, Pope Francis asked, What can Christians do today in light of so many divisions? Will people simply resign themselves to the current state of affairs and give up, becoming indifferent, "or will we firmly believe that one can and must walk in the direction of reconciliation and full communion? Let theologians debate and discuss the issues at hand and seek the theological truth because it is a duty," he said. "But we will walk together, praying for one another, doing charitable work, and that is how we will build our communion."[8]

As he notes, spiritual ecumenism is by no means limited to prayer. As the Decree on Ecumenism noted, it calls us to a change of heart "for it is from newness of attitudes of mind, from self-denial and unstinted love, that desires of unity take their rise and develop in a mature way. We should therefore pray to the Holy Spirit for the grace to be genuinely self-denying, humble, gentle in the service of others, and to have an attitude of brotherly generosity toward them" (no. 7).

Other attitudes of heart and mind involved in the practice of spiritual ecumenism are:

- Repentance
- Appreciation of particular spiritual gifts and practices found in various churches
- Honesty and charity in dealings with the other
- Coherence between what we say and what we do
- Attentiveness to the place of ecumenical friendship in our spiritual journeys
- Curiosity about the other
- Humility—an active virtue demanding repeated examination of conscience
- Patience and impatience (patience—with the glacier-like slowness of unity efforts; impatience for a more credible and vitalizing gospel witness in the life of the churches to the power of God to reconcile)
- Christian hope

Over the course of my fourteen years working at the Canadian Centre for Ecumenism, I saw the need for more places where Christians from different traditions could come together for days at a time to share faith and life, to pray with one another, and engage in the exchange of spiritual gifts. So I became involved in the work of founding Unitas, an ecumenical center for spirituality cosponsored by eight different denominations in Montreal. By the time I left Unitas five years later, in response to the Paulist community's call to develop a Paulist North American Office for Ecumenical and Interfaith Relations in the United States, the total combined annual enrollment in our prayer gatherings, programs, and retreats surpassed nine thousand. It met a need.

The approach we took at Unitas was one of spiritual ecumenism. The time spent together in faith sharing and prayer, the spiritual gifts exchanged, transformed peoples' perceptions of one another and enriched their lives in concrete and lasting ways. It was a way of engaging in the work for Christian unity that moved on the level of church members and had a direct, positive impact on their lives and their subsequent witness and prayer.

MARGARET'S STORY

The ecumenical community of Taizé in southern France has become known around the world for its style of song-prayer in which a concise verse is chanted repeatedly for several minutes, with periods of silence between the songs. One of the practices that characterizes prayer on Friday nights at Taizé is prayer around the cross. While the congregation engages in the meditative chants, every person is welcome to come and kneel around the large cross laid on the floor and touch it or place their forehead upon it in prayer. At Unitas, in our monthly Friday evening of prayer in the style of Taizé, we followed the same practice. It's a form of meditative prayer in community that takes people to a very deep place inside themselves and gives them a taste of inner stillness. And in that silence, they come to rest in God. My theory is that one of the main reasons Taizé prayer continues to draw people is that it has never lost sight of what people yearn for most: an experience of God. A story shared by a Unitas retreatant, Margaret O'Donnell, reveals how far-reaching the impact of spiritual ecumenism can be.

I would like to tell you the story of how the Spirit brought about a shift in my own heart, one that helped me to imagine that the impossible could become possible in my own setting, my community, my town. Sometimes we are slow to see the ecumenical possibilities existing inside our neighborhoods and that the experience of unity that Jesus desires for his followers is already available to ourselves and to our neighbors.

I was a visitor to Montreal and to Unitas. The memory is clear: an invitation to participate in a Unitas ecumenical service—the Friday night Taizé Prayer around the Cross. Mid-point in the service, one is invited to place one's forehead on the wood of the cross, and in so doing, shift the burdens of one's heart to the cross. Taizé brothers were taught this gesture, I learned, inside a Russian prison, by those imprisoned for their faith. That Friday night at Unitas, I placed my forehead on the cross, and my consciousness shifted to the agony of the whole world, and the question stirred: "How can this form of prayer come to my town, Victoria, in British Columbia?"

The particular reason my story is extra challenging is that I knew about the practical ecumenism of Taizé, and of how this monastic endeavor belonged, not to any one denomination, but to all. How could churches come together, each on an equal footing with the other, so that, as at Taizé, no single denomination would "own" the initiative, but rather together, as a communion of denominations, we would forge a new unity that we would express in a common prayer? The God of the Future found me in my blindness, and led me forward, one small step at a time.

Fall, 1995: Back in Victoria, people pointed me toward others, like the Christian bookstore owner, who said: "Lucia and Brother Jean Louis were by. Both were asking if Taizé prayer occurs in Victoria?" Then there was Don, the United Church minister, who suggested a conversation with Fran, the choir director for the Metropolitan United Church. Fran, who said "Talk to Jackie, the choir director for St. Andrew's Cathedral Choirs."

Winter, 1996: Jackie, Fran and I meet in a Japanese restaurant, and crafted a response to John, the Dean of the

Anglican Christ Church Cathedral and Chair of the Downtown Churches Association (DCA) who'd sent a message: "Please, we want Prayer in the style of Taizé, each day at noon, during the week of Prayer for Christian Unity." Further restaurant lunches, and we came up with a formal request to the Victoria Downtown Churches Association (DCA) to sponsor our now shared "dream": Prayer around the cross in the style of Taizé, monthly from September to June, with three different churches per year hosting it on a rotating basis.

Spring, 1996: John and the DCA probed us with questions to discern our motives and intentions and then— joy! Approval was given to launch the first May, 1996 DCA-sponsored Prayer in the Style of Taizé, hosted by Metropolitan United Church.

Since then, and for close to nineteen years now, we have been "guest" and "host" in one another's church homes, discovering the architecture, corporate personality, and personal face of each denomination, through the welcome and hospitality of each church-home.

To stabilize the initiative for the good of all, Lucia, Jean Louis and I formed a council. On Saturday mornings, following the prayer service, I would ring people up, both guests and hosts, and inquire "What went well? What was challenging? For what are you grateful about last night's prayer?" Synthesis of this input formed the basis of our council discussion. With time, this council expanded to include the musicians, who had important questions and input. The council worked toward a goal to build a mandate into the job description of musicians from the downtown churches to offer musical leadership when their church was hosting the monthly prayer service.

As time went on, the prayer service took root among the downtown churches within five denominations: Anglican, Roman Catholic, United, Lutheran, and Reformed, with occasional Ukrainian Catholic participation as well. We faced the question: How do we stabilize this initiative so that it is not the work of any one person, or denomination? With the expansion came the need to grow the council, today called the steering committee, composed of a delegation from each denomination which gathers quarterly in friendship to determine the rotation and evaluate any needs. Past chairpersons form a discernment committee to aid the steering committee in its selection of a new chairperson. Down the years, chairpersons have arisen from within the Roman Catholic, United, First Nation, and Anglican communities. From time to time, Brother Emile from Taizé comes among us for a time of renewal. His presence renews bonds that go back through years and to our origins.

What have been the fruits? Praying together is doubtless the greatest fruit. Those of us at the core of this initiative have come to know each other well, in respectful, trusting and long-term relationships born from belonging, yes, to an individual denomination, but even more deeply, to an authentic existential experience of unity between denominations expressed in concrete ways at the grassroots level. Essential to the creative unfolding of the monthly prayer service was solid working relations with each preparation team, which included the pastor, the secretary, the musicians, the sacristan, the flower arrangers, the verger, and above all, the janitor (who held the key to the storage room, and assured timely and efficient building openings and closures).

My story brings me back to a shift that took place in my heart at Unitas in Montreal, and then to my blindness in knowing how to go forward. In the founding years, I came to know that the impossible could become possible only by a shift in myself. The work, I detected, was to open to the unique gift of our unity, and to confirm each denomination in the eyes of the wider community of faith. With time and trust, the truth that became equally evident was that just as each denomination possessed a gift, so no denomination was without its agony, its cross. The shift required was to recognize that my heart belonged to both the gift and the poverty of each community, and I laid my forehead on the cross of suffering at the heart of each one's story.

How deeply I give thanks for the rich experience of ecumenism our churches have provided our neighborhoods. I send a message of thanks as well to the Taizé community in France and to Unitas in Montreal, for the role of each in inspiring our nineteen-year journey as a Communion of communions.

There are various insights offered in Margaret's story. How the Holy Spirit's movement in one person's heart can have a domino effect when one is responsive to it. How spiritual ecumenism can have devotional, dialogical, and organizational dimensions. How in prayer together the undivided church becomes visible, not only as a distant memory of the first millennium, but also as a reality that is there today and needs to be rediscovered and made increasingly visible. This is the best experience Christian faith has to offer: simple communion in love.

OTHER FORMS OF SPIRITUAL ECUMENISM

My years at Unitas provided me with experience in leading ecumenical retreats and only sharpened my appetite for more. That particular form of spiritual ecumenism continues to play a large role in the deployment of my time and energy. The retreats are offered on themes with broad and popular appeal: Together in Christ; Cultivating a Holistic Spirituality; Prayer of Heart and Body; Savoring Life in Every Season; Pray All Ways; Becoming Free; Lessons from the Mystics; Contemplative Prayer in the Christian Tradition; Challenge and Inspiration from Other Religions; and Accessing Your Creativity.[9]

People come from different traditions of Christian faith and engage in a weekend or weeklong period of sharing their faith and life experience, praying together, singing in harmony, learning and drawing inspiration from one another, and experiencing the richness of inhabiting periods of silence in community. As St. John Paul II said in his encyclical letter, *That All May Be One*, "Even when prayer is not specifically offered for Christian unity, but for other intentions such as peace, it actually becomes an expression and confirmation of unity. The common prayer of Christians is an invitation to Christ himself to visit the community of those who call upon him: 'Where two or three are gathered in my name, there am I in the midst of them' (Matt 18:20)" (*Ut Unum Sint* 21).

Coming into the retreat, their perception of one another as Catholic or Protestant or Evangelical or Orthodox may have simply been shaped by social stereotypes from their upbringing. However, after sharing faith in prayer or over meals or in groups, after experiencing each other's love of the Lord up close, by the time they leave, a relationship has been created, contact information is exchanged, and the former stranger is now recognized as a brother or sister in the Lord.

Another expression for me of spiritual ecumenism is preaching cosponsored, four-day congregational faith renewal events called Gospel Call with a Protestant preaching partner, Rev. John Armstrong. On Sunday, we split up and preach in as many of the cosponsoring churches as is logistically possible. Then we preach together on Sunday, Monday, and Tuesday nights.

Each evening, the Service of the Word is held in a different church to provide participants with an opportunity to pray together in one another's worship spaces. The pastor of the hosting church presides; the missioners (my partner and I) preach and lead all participants in a ritual action emphasizing the commonality of our faith and in accord with the theme of that particular evening's scriptural readings.

The fellowship dimension is integral. On Sunday evening, preceding the evening service, there is a potluck supper, jointly sponsored and organized by the participating congregations. On Monday, Tuesday, and Wednesday, following the evening services, everyone is invited to gather in the hosting congregation's fellowship hall for refreshments and socializing.

Once during the course of each weekday, a different spiritual growth and development opportunity is offered in the form of a breakfast workshop for people on their way to work in the morning, a mid-morning Bible study, and an afternoon session on the gifts that the different churches have to share with one another for their mutual enrichment. Similarly, these sessions are located in the various churches to provide people with an opportunity to become comfortable entering into one another's churches.

On the last evening, Wednesday, people who are engaged in similar ministries in the various cosponsoring congregations come together—youth ministry, liturgy and music, administration, social action, and Christian education. In a session that begins and ends with prayer, representatives from the cosponsoring churches are invited to share with one another in break-out groups what they do, the resources they find helpful in their particular area of ministry, and whether there are any ways they can support one another's efforts or act together. This input provides direction for ongoing collaboration between the local churches as they face the future. The number of cosponsoring congregations can be as few as three or as many as ten.[10]

Of all the ministerial engagements I have been blessed to participate in over the years, the ecumenical retreats and Gospel Call are the most fulfilling. Their correlation with spiritual and receptive ecumenism is rich and direct.

The ecumenical movement is not only an exchange of ideas and documents, nor only a matter of working side by side to overcome poverty and racism; it is also an exchange of spiritual gifts and spiritual experiences. It no longer starts with what divides us, but with what we have in common. It starts with common Christian experiences and with common Christian challenges in our more or less secularized and multicultural world.

Spiritual ecumenism must seek out and serve life. It must be concerned with everyday human experiences as well as with the great questions of justice and peace and the preservation of creation. Through the prayer and the sharing, our hearts are turned more fully toward Christ, and the closer we come to him, the more we discover ourselves in unity. And in the exchange of gifts, what is lacking in each of our traditions finds its needed complement. The ecumenical endeavor thus becomes a pilgrimage to the fullness of catholicity that Jesus Christ intends for his church.

WHAT SPIRITUAL ECUMENISM DOES NOT MEAN

These reflections on spiritual ecumenism should not be taken to imply that we're giving up on any significant change in the structural relationships between the churches or in their theology and teaching. Neither does it mean that we resign ourselves to peaceful coexistence in division and simply remember each other occasionally in prayer. What it does mean is that all ecumenical work ultimately finds fruition in the spiritual realm, that is, in and through the Holy Spirit.[11]

We can affirm that many prejudices and misunderstandings of the past have been overcome, that bridges of new mutual understanding and practical cooperation have been built. We can affirm that in many cases convergences and consensus have been found. Examples here would be baptism and Eucharist, the relationship between Scripture and Tradition, justification by faith, the nature of the church. And other differences have been better identified and explored, such as the Petrine ministry or ethical questions relating to the nature of marriage and sexuality.

Let us say it again: The work for Christian unity has nothing to do with syncretism or finding a lowest common denominator. It has to do with full visible communion in faith, sacramental life, apostolic ministry, and mission. Full communion does not mean uniformity, but exists alongside cultural diversity, alongside different liturgical rites, different forms of piety, different but complementary emphases and perspectives.[12]

As Cardinal Walter Kasper has stated:

> There is no reason to be discouraged or frustrated, or to speak of an "ecumenical winter." The Spirit who initiated the ecumenical movement has also accompanied it and made it fruitful. We have achieved more than we could have imagined or dreamed forty years ago. Yet we must also admit, realistically, that we have not yet reached the goal of our ecumenical pilgrimage, but are still at an intermediate stage. There remain fundamental problems to solve and differences to overcome.[13]

RECEPTIVE ECUMENISM

How can the various traditions of Christian faith more genuinely and effectively learn or receive from one another with integrity, *now*? How can we keep the momentum going in this intermediate stage when the hope for more ministerial, sacramental, and structural unity is now widely seen as being unrealistic? The third phase in the ecumenical movement is the strategy of "receptive ecumenism." Phases one and two are the traditional complementary forms of Christian unity efforts represented in the Life and Work and Faith and Order Movements.

The Life and Work Movement emerged from the groundbreaking 1910 Edinburgh World Missionary Conference and sought to bring the churches from mutual hostility and mistrust to recognition and effective collaboration in worship, work, and mission. As an "ecumenism of life," it would later represent one of the key foundational stones for the establishment of the World Council of Churches (WCC) in 1948. Its core concern was to develop a shared relationship and feet-on-the-ground practical cooperation between formerly divided traditions of Christian faith.

Ecumenism's second phase, the Faith and Order movement, also evolved from the Edinburgh gathering. It sought to address the institutional, ministerial, and sacramental divisions that have perdured over centuries. It brought to bear an "ecumenism of dialogue" on formal doctrinal and ecclesiological causes of division, and it also served as a keystone undertaking in the creation of the WCC.

When the Catholic Church formally entered into the ecumenical movement following the Second Vatican Council and invested strongly in national and international dialogues, the progress on this level was such that it fed ballooning expectations about the possible realization of full structural, sacramental, and ministerial communion within a generation. In contrast, however, to those heady days, the high wave of reconciliation through theological dialogue and clarification appears to have crashed on the beach, leaving some of the great dialogue documents as the high-water mark of a tide now turned. We now realize that we are dealing with substantive, long-term differences that, at the formal level, are not going to be resolved for the foreseeable future. There is no denying that over the past decade or so, formal ecumenism has experienced an energy drain with the surfacing of significant doctrinal issues not easily resolved, leaving the movement for unity in a place of apparent impasse.[14]

How are we to live in the interim, not giving up on the vision, not tempted to settle for less? How might we learn and receive from one another in this middle time with its challenges and problems?

It is precisely in this period that receptive ecumenism has emerged as a new strategy. Pioneered in recent years through a series of projects in England operating out of Durham University's Department of Theology and Religion, and given momentum by international conferences devoted to it in 2006, 2009, and 2014, receptive ecumenism proceeds by bringing to the fore the dispositions of hospitality, humble learning, and ongoing conversion that have always been quietly essential to good ecumenical work. Receptive ecumenism turns those dispositions into an explicit strategy and a core task.[15]

Receptive ecumenism seeks to cultivate within us the *necessary prior desire* for deeper relationship with other Christians that the formal dialogues between our churches presuppose and without which their work will never come to fruition. That necessary prior desire is the work of the Holy Spirit, an inclination of our hearts that finds delight in another's gifts and beauties, that is able to recognize a fitting match between our particular lacks and needs and the other's particular gifts.[16]

The message that Catholics might learn and receive from other Christian communities had already been sent in the Decree on Ecumenism: "From time to time, one tradition has come nearer to a full appreciation of some aspects of a mystery of revelation than the other, or has expressed it to better advantage. In such cases, these various theological expressions are to be considered often as mutually complementary rather than conflicting" (no. 17).

The primary call of receptive ecumenism is to take responsibility for one's own and one's own community's learning, without first demanding that the other do likewise. Instead of approaching the other, thinking, *What do they need to learn from us?*, we ask, *What is it that we need to and can learn from them? How are we moving into holy ground when we move into one another's presence?* Required is a fundamental shift from each tradition of Christian faith assertively defending its own perceived inheritance in competition with each other, to taking responsibility for its own potential learning from others.[17]

While one can always hope that the other will also respond to the call to receptive ecumenical learning, and while one can always be prepared to contribute to such a process if asked to do so, this can never be made a prior condition for taking responsibility for one's own and one's community's learning. So much for the better if our own good practice in relation to Catholicism serves in turn to encourage members of other traditions to embark upon and embrace similar initiatives for themselves! In doing so, we witness to how difference can be a grace and blessing for mutual flourishing. In other words, the ethic at work in receptive ecumenism is one wherein each tradition takes responsibility for its own potential learning from others and is, in turn, willing to facilitate the learning of others as requested, but without making this a precondition to attending to one's own. In short, learning will take precedence over teaching.[18]

Receptive ecumenism represents a long-term learning opportunity in which the churches can progress toward their calling and destiny. It's an essential way forward toward the anticipated goal of organic unity. The therapeutic adage is apt: "We cannot change others. We can only change ourselves"—and, thereby, the way we relate to others. This approach alters things and opens up new possibilities. The heart of receptive ecumenism is moving away from wishing that others could be more like us, to instead asking what we can and must learn from the other.[19]

In a series of engagements in Saskatoon, Saskatchewan, Paul Murray, the director for the Centre for Catholic Studies at Durham University in England and a leader in shaping and promoting receptive ecumenism internationally, explained his vision of this strategy as a way to both enhance and continue the journey of Christian unity. He acknowledged that what is being proposed here is conversion—not from one tradition to another, but the more fundamental call to Christian conversion involving an ever-deepening insertion into the fullness of Christ.

> We are each wounded…and what we need to do is to be prepared—now that we have built a relationship—to trust that we are now moving into the more challenging and also potentially the more life-giving possibility of showing

those wounds to each other, knowing that we cannot heal ourselves, and asking that the other minister to our needs.

Speaking as a Catholic, my hope for Catholicism through receptive ecumenism is not that we will become less Catholic. My hope is that we will become more Catholic—more richly, more deeply, more utterly Catholic—precisely by becoming more connectional from Methodism, perhaps more synodal from Orthodoxy and Anglicanism. And from the Lutherans, learning really what it means to take justification by faith seriously, recognizing moment by moment we stand under the forgiving and empowering way of God.[20]

In short, receptive ecumenism is about coming to a positive appreciation for the presence and action of God in the people, practices, structures, and processes of another tradition and being impelled thereby to search for ways in which all impediments to our closer relationship might be overcome. This has the effect of expanding our possibilities and stimulating the process of ecclesial growth and conversion.

This strategy is guided both by theological principle and practical insight. The theological principle is that if the call to full, visible communion is really a gospel imperative, then the fresh challenges being faced by us in the ecumenical journey should not be read as an insuperable roadblock or as arrival at the end of the road. In Christian understanding, God can be trusted to provide us with the resources needed to respond to God's call to unity and to live that call fruitfully in any given context. There must be a fitting means of continuing to walk toward and to live in anticipation of the reality of full communion.[21]

This approach views the churches collectively as each being on a long-term path to ecclesial renewal and growth: in short, of being in a state of *semper reformandi* ("always reforming") as Martin Luther put it, or in a state of *semper purificanda* ("always purifying itself") as the Second Vatican Council's Dogmatic Constitution on the Church, *Lumen Gentium*, expressed it. In this perspective, the longer-term ecumenical journey on which the churches are embarked, and the recalibration of ecumenical expectation that this evokes, is not a case of earlier poor judgment on our part as to what is possible. It is a consequence of the softwood having been cut through and the hardwood now being engaged. The only route possible now is that of grace-filled learning as to how we are all being called to grow to a new place where new things become possible.[22] The gospel always calls us to greater life and flourishing. We should not be surprised that, across the whole of our lives, there is change and growth, intensification and enrichment.

Complementing these theological convictions are some pragmatic principles and insights. During the same period that the churches have come to see the fulfillment of the ecumenical goal as being on a slower track than once envisaged, they have also come to more sober evaluations of their respective shortcomings, challenges, and needs. Each tradition has its own specific difficulties that it can be incapable of resolving from its own existing resources. Opening to refreshment and renewal from without, to alternative approaches and ecclesial experiences of other traditions, can become a dynamic process that will take each tradition to new places for their own respective health and flourishing. This reflects a move *away* from ideal, theorized, purely doctrinally driven ecclesiological constructs in ecumenical dialogue and a definite move *toward* taking the lived reality more seriously. As each tradition opens to learn and receive from associated understandings and practices of other traditions, there will be a life-giving move toward a more honest assessment of where the specific difficulties in their own tradition lie and how they might fruitfully learn in these regards, with appropriate testing, from other traditions.[23]

Theology professor and noted ecumenist Dr. Catherine Clifford, from St. Paul University in Ottawa, shares her observation of Pope Francis relative to receptive ecumenism:[24]

Pope Francis seems to grasp intuitively the need for receptive ecumenism and ecumenical learning. If he does not use the terminology, his discourse and actions, nonetheless, invite an active attentiveness to gifts and potential areas of learning which address our ecclesial needs. In his Apostolic Exhortation on the Joy of the Gospel, he maintains: "If we really believe in the abundantly free working of the Holy Spirit, we can learn so much from one another! It is not just about being better informed about others, but rather about reaping what the Spirit has sown in them, which is also meant to be a gift for us."[25]

It is significant that he makes this statement in the context of a much wider call for a comprehensive "pastoral and missionary conversion" of the structures and practices of the Catholic Church in view of a more effective witness and proclamation of the gospel in the world today. The restoration of ecclesial unity is not an end in itself but is essential to the credibility of the church's witness. Pope Francis has understood that Christians need each other to carry out the mission of the church in the world today.

Citing the example of dialogue with the Orthodox Churches, he observes, "we Catholics have the opportunity to learn more about the meaning of episcopal collegiality and their experience of synodality. Through an exchange of gifts, the Spirit can lead us ever more fully into truth and goodness."[26] While the Second Vatican Council may have drawn our attention to these ideas, it is fair to say that they have yet to be fully received or given concrete expression in Catholic ecclesial life. Three areas for Catholic ecumenical learning stand out as having profound implications for the future of ecclesial communion: the primacy of the Bishop of Rome; the collegial exercise of the episcopal office as an expression of communion between the local churches; and the dignity of the laity.

Receptive ecumenism offers a constructive way ahead in a situation where some of the dialogues seem to have run out of steam. It starts with humble recognition of the wounds, tears, and difficulties in one's own tradition and asks how the particular and different gifts, experiences, and ways of proceeding in the other traditions can speak to and help to heal these wounds. Receptive ecumenism represents a way forward in which the currently divided traditions can walk toward full structural, ministerial, sacramental communion and their own healing together.[27]

Thus, in this intermediate season that we are presently in, the answer is not to move toward a lesser goal of reconciled diversity without structural and sacramental unity, but rather to envision how Christian traditions might more genuinely and effectively learn or receive from one another with integrity, *now*.

Reconciled diversity without structural and sacramental unity can simply never be a sufficient equivalent to the intended unity and catholicity of the church. The forms of structural unity that appropriately reflect this calling will necessarily be a long haul. But to give up on it for that reason would be like giving up on the aspiration for economic justice that will likewise be a long haul. The point is to ask what it means to live now oriented toward such goals.

One could say that the bringing of all things into fully actualized, differentiated communion in God is an end-time reality. But Christian existence is properly viewed as living from the vision of and toward this proper end. As such, the point is not to relegate it to the irrelevant future but to live in the light of it, anticipating it and being drawn into it as fully as possible amidst present conditions. From this perspective, the Christian task is not so much to construct the kingdom as to lean into its coming, to be shaped and formed in accordance with it so as to become a concrete expression of its anticipatory realization in the world.[28]

Our tendency for making judicious and calculated assessments of the possibilities for movement toward unity can easily translate into losing our capacity for Christian hope. We keep trying to trim God's reconciling mandate down to our limited imaginings, but the vision of Christian unity God has put before us is expansive. Big dreams call for big hopes.[29]

God guarantees a good outcome, but without telling us what it will be. As Vatican II affirmed in its Decree on Ecumenism, this holy objective—the reconciliation of all Christians in the unity of the one and only church of Christ—transcends human powers and gifts (no. 24). The Holy Spirit is the originator of the movement for union and communion, and the Spirit remains in charge of it: "It is the Holy Spirit, dwelling in those who believe and pervading and ruling over the entire church, who brings about that wonderful communion of the faithful and joins them together so intimately in Christ that he is the principle of the church's unity" (no. 2).

As Pope John Paul II wrote in his apostolic letter "At the Beginning of a New Millennium," "It is on Jesus' prayer and not on our own strength that we base the hope that even within history we shall be able to reach full and visible communion with all Christians."[30] In that letter, he developed what he called "a spirituality of communion."

> To make the Church *the home and the school of communion*: that is the great challenge facing us in the millennium which is now beginning, if we wish to be faithful to God's plan and respond to the world's deepest yearnings.
>
> But what does this mean in practice? Here too, our thoughts could run immediately to the action to be undertaken, but that would not be the right impulse to follow. Before making practical plans, we need *to promote a spirituality of communion*, making it the guiding principle of education wherever individuals and Christians are formed, wherever ministers of the altar, consecrated persons, and pastoral workers are trained, wherever families and communities are being built up.
>
> A spirituality of communion indicates above all the heart's contemplation of the mystery of the Trinity dwelling in us, and whose light we must also be able to see shining on the face of the brothers and sisters around us. A spirituality of communion also means an ability to think of our brothers and sisters in faith within the profound unity of the Mystical Body, and therefore as "those who are a part of me." This makes us share their joys and sufferings, to sense their desires and attend to their needs, to offer them deep and genuine friendship. A spirituality of communion implies also the ability to see what is positive in others, to welcome it and prize it as a gift from God: not only as a gift for the brother or sister who has received directly, but also as a "gift for me." A spirituality of communion means, finally, to know how to "make room" for our brothers and sisters, bearing "each other's burdens" (Gal 6:2) and resisting the selfish temptations which constantly beset us and provoke competition,

careerism, distrust and jealousy. Let us have no illusions: unless we follow this spiritual path, external structures of communion will serve very little purpose. They would become mechanisms without a soul, masks of communion rather than as a means of expression and growth.[31]

This spirituality of communion through an exchange of spiritual gifts and experiences will move all parties toward the concrete fullness of catholicity. The aim is mutual spiritual enrichment. The aim is discovering the truth of the other as our own truth, and being led by the Spirit into the whole truth.

So the question is this: What might we have to learn from other Christian traditions? In the next chapter, we'll examine closely some of the particular spiritual gifts offered by the different traditions of Christian faith to one another for their mutual enrichment.

9. GIFTS TO SHARE FOR OUR MUTUAL ENRICHMENT

The Second Vatican Council embraced a vision of ecclesial unity that has come to be described as a communion/*koinonia* of diverse churches, bound together by a common faith that is enriched by a legitimate diversity of expression in liturgy, theology, spirituality, and canonical structure.[1]

Starting with the sacramental bond of baptism, the Council seeks to affirm the communion that we already share in Christ in consequence of our being incorporated into the one church of Christ. In acknowledging that the churches have at times followed different paths and methods, the Decree on Ecumenism nonetheless affirms that "from time to time one tradition has come nearer to a full appreciation of some aspects of a mystery of revelation than the other, or has expressed them better. In such cases, these various theological formulations are often to be considered complementary rather than conflicting" (no. 17).

These teachings indicate that Catholics might learn and receive from other Christian communities an insight that Pope Francis has been promoting as well. The Catholic Church made a fundamental shift in its vision of Christian unity from Vatican I to Vatican II, moving from an ecumenism of "return" to an ecumenism of "recognition"—the recognition of an esteem for the many gifts of God's Spirit that reflect a genuine communion of faith and life with other Christian churches.[2]

In short, the Council calls Catholics to respect and reverence the "riches of Christ" in fellow Christians. To remember that what the Holy Spirit accomplishes in separated brothers and sisters can contribute to our own growth and deepening as Christians and even as "a more ample realization of the very mystery of Christ and the Church" (Decree on Ecumenism 4).

In "A Church in Dialogue," the Canadian Catholic Bishops, quoting Pope John Paul II and Pope Francis, acknowledge that certain features of the Christian mystery have at times been more effectively emphasized in other Christian communities.

> Pope John Paul II gave the Church a language for the notion of learning from other Christian Communities when he noted that ecumenical dialogue "is not simply an exchange of ideas. In some way it is always an 'exchange of gifts'" (*That All May Be One*, no. 28). He expressed confidence that an exchange of gifts has already been taking place in recent decades, and spoke of how ecumenical dialogue "works to awaken a reciprocal fraternal assistance, whereby Communities strive to give in mutual exchange what each one needs in order to grow towards definitive fullness in accordance with God's plan," providing an "ecumenical expression of the Gospel law of sharing" (*That All May Be One*, no. 87).
>
> Pope Francis has taken this a step further, inviting an active attentiveness to gifts in the order of potential areas of learning that address our own ecclesial needs. "If we really believe in the abundantly free working of the Holy Spirit, we can learn so much from one another! It is not just about being better informed about others, but rather about reaping what the Spirit has sown in them, which is also meant to be a gift for us" (*The Joy of the Gospel*, no. 246).[3]

In the spirit of recognition and mutual enrichment, I will lift up five gifts each from five confessional families—Protestant, Anglican, Pentecostal, Orthodox, and Roman Catholic—which might bring Christians mutually to fuller flourishing.[4] This list is by no means exhaustive and its scope is modest. Rather than focusing on the entire range of church life and organization, its focus is on *spiritual* gifts, primarily because I want to focus on those things that are within our learning capabilities as individuals. My desire is only to stimulate reflection, appreciation, and spiritual growth.

PROTESTANT

Protestantism's contributions of both personal and communal forms of spirituality to the Christian treasure chest are varied and rich.[5] Among them are

1) *Free expression and spontaneity in prayer*: With some exceptions (for example, charismatics), Christians from the so-called "liturgical traditions"—Lutherans, Anglicans, Roman Catholics, and Orthodox—rely on prayer formulas when they pray together and seem to feel generally out of their matrix when invited to pray extemporaneously. One Catholic layman who directed the Parish Renew program in his diocese identified three particular fruits among the participating parishioners: they met new people in the parish, they got more familiar with their Bibles, and they began to learn how to pray together without written formulas.

2) *Scripture reading* often accompanies prayer and is the primary source on which prayer is based in Protestant spirituality. Benedictines and other monastic communities have their "Rule" of life, but for Protestants the "rule" is the Bible. The scriptures were made the focal point for all people early on through translation into the vernacular, and meditation upon the scriptures has deep roots in the tradition. The plethora of Scripture study materials for daily use among Catholics today (*The Word among Us*; *Give Us This Day*; *Magnificat*; *Living Faith*, to cite but four available in North America) is a wonderful example of the reception of gifts from one another.

3) *Hymn writing and singing* are important forms of Protestant spirituality. The hymns serve as devotional expression, catechetical instruction, and the facilitation of congregational participation in worship. Protestants' ready inclination to sing their faith leaves me consistently envious of that richness in their tradition. On Sunday morning

in Catholic Churches, even when there are books in the pews and a music group or choir to lead, I see many worshippers standing with their arms folded, content to leave the singing to others. I once led a weekend retreat for Mennonites in which every conference and every meal was initiated with song-prayers in four-part harmony and there wasn't a sheet of music in sight. Many Protestant congregations now have what they call "blended worship"—encompassing both traditional and contemporary forms of music in the same service or having one service in a more traditional style and another in a more contemporary one.

4) *An understanding of the church as the whole people of God and ministry as the priesthood of all believers*: One of the richest expressions of this historically was the identification of the family as a worthy context for one's spiritual quest. In Luther's eyes, one of the greatest acts of devotion and one of the most rewarding Christian vocations was to be a pastor to one's family. In many ways, the home became the alternative to the monastery, a little church, a natural matrix in which the Christian could live out and witness to his/her faith. In John Bunyan's classic *Pilgrim's Progress*, the pilgrims visited homes and families, not churches, on their journey.

5) As the list of gifts is too long to be constrained to a list of five, let me simply list some very attractive features that often characterize, for example, Evangelical Christians and/or their congregations:
   a) Strong emphasis on a personal relationship with Christ
   b) Readiness to share one's faith story
   c) Programs for youth with both social and faith dimensions
   d) Fellowship/hospitality/welcome
   e) Missionary spirituality, for example, the Great Commission to "go make disciples" is for everyone, along with an active sense of discipleship to one's family and community.

ANGLICAN

Many of the new Anglican formularies of the mid-sixteenth century corresponded closely to those of contemporary Reformed Protestantism. However, by the end of the sixteenth century, the retention in Anglicanism of many traditional liturgical forms and of the episcopate was already seen as unacceptable by those promoting the most developed Protestant principles. In the first half of the seventeenth century, the Church of England and associated Episcopal Churches in Ireland and in England's American colonies were presented by some Anglican divines as comprising a distinct Christian Tradition, with theologies, structures, and forms of worship representing a middle ground between Reformed Protestantism and Roman Catholicism; a perspective that came to be highly influential in later theories of Anglican identity. Some distinctive gifts that Anglicans bring are

1) *Prayer texts and liturgical style*: In the United States during the 1940s, members of the Catholic Vernacular Society proposed adopting the *Book of Common Prayer* as a base text for Roman Catholic worship in English because of its beautifully crafted and theologically rich prayer texts. In terms of style, Anglican worship demonstrates well that it is possible to celebrate a participative, reformed liturgy without losing a sense of reverence and mystery in worship.

2) *Non-eucharistic forms of liturgy*: Anglicans have been successful at sustaining and promoting ancient non-eucharistic forms of liturgy such as Morning and Evening Prayer. The Council of Trent (1545–63) and the Second Vatican Council (1962–65) made various attempts to encourage laity to join their clergy in praying Sunday Vespers together, but without notable fruit. In Anglicanism, by contrast, one finds the rich musical tradition of Evensong with its numerous beautiful settings of the Psalms, the *Magnificat*, the *Nunc Dimittis*, and the glorious anthems sung by choirs in Anglican churches throughout the world.

3) *Effective participation of clergy and laypeople in decision making*: In the first millennium, the church functioned with collegial structures of synodality and consultation not unlike what one finds today throughout the Anglican Communion. Laypeople were also active participants with clergy in the choice of bishops. Within Anglicanism, there is a strong commitment to synodal structures at all levels of church life. This is a feature of church life that also characterizes the Orthodox and mainline Protestant traditions.

4) *The ability to live with the questions in an open, honest, and transparent way*: Anglicans exhibit a willingness to engage in difficult questions, to set forth all of the arguments—from Scripture, from Tradition, from reason (drawing on contemporary scholarship in diverse fields), and from experience (including those who find themselves marginalized)—in order to discern a way forward. To quote one Anglican, "Anglicans insist on washing their dirty laundry in public. But at least we wash it!" At times, this can appear as a gift, at times, as something approaching internal chaos with the result of strains upon internal unity. Some would undoubtedly favor safeguarding unity by closing down discussion on controversial issues, but is it not naïve to avoid the questions, hoping they will go away? Anglicans demonstrate the gift of asking questions that need to be asked.

5) *A capacity for dialogue with other religious traditions*: The Anglican Communion offers us a wonderful example in the initiative of the former Archbishop of Canterbury, Dr. George Carey, in opening an ongoing dialogue with Muslims. Appropriately called "Building Bridges," this initiative was carried forth by his successors, Rowan Williams and now Justin Welby. Each spring, Christian and Muslim scholars gather together at the Jesuit University of Georgetown in Washington, DC, for their deliberations. The depth of commitment among those who are involved in that dialogue is already beginning to bear fruit in terms of increased Muslim and Christian scholarly collaboration.

It is instinctual for Anglicans to think to include scholars who are not Anglican, so that Christians of different churches can work together on the dialogue and can also be seen by the dialogue partners as working together.

PENTECOSTAL

The particular feature of Pentecostal identity is the unique emphasis on the person, work, and gifts of the Holy Spirit. Worldwide, Pentecostalism is the fastest growing Christian denomination. In 2011, a Pew Forum study of global Christianity found that there were an estimated 279 million classical Pentecostals, 12.8 percent of the world's Christian population.[6] What are their particular contributions?

1) *The revalorization of the gifts of the Holy Spirit* is the greatest gift of this movement. Until recently, the Western church has more or less held that the miraculous and extraordinary gifts of the Spirit were withdrawn after the gospel had been authenticated under the apostles. Most Protestants have taught that this withdrawal came with the final resolution of the canon of Scripture. However, since 1901, the prevalence of such charisms as glossolalia (speaking in tongues), divine healing, and exorcism has been the hallmark of Pentecostalism around the world. Pentecostalism, in its apocalyptic freshness and comparative youth, explores ways to rekindle the passion that has marked it from the beginning and still irrupts in its midst. The manifestation of spiritual gifts often reveals the presence of satanic forces, and the church in recent years has come to a renewed understanding of the reality of spiritual warfare.

2) *Enthusiastic and expressive worship* that is often accompanied with singing in tongues, applause to the Lord, the raising of hands, and the shouting of loud "amens" and "alleluias." The expressive worship of Pentecostalism is often embraced by people who desire "heart religion" over more literary and intellectual forms of faith and worship. In Latin and African cultures in particular, spiritual dancing

accompanies the singing. The number of people from historic churches going to their assemblies for worship asks us whether we are too cerebral in our services and do not appeal enough to the heart.

3) *Concert prayer* is the standard form for most Pentecostal and charismatic groups. It is a general time of prayer in which the entire congregation prays together loudly "in concert." This is in contrast to traditional modes of prayer that are led by one person, usually the pastor. Spontaneous and extemporaneous prayer by pastors or prayer group leaders, in contrast to formalized written prayers, has entered strongly into the mainstream of the churches and is one of the contributions of Pentecostalism to the whole church.

4) *The cost of discipleship*: We could all learn something about recruitment from the Pentecostals. Participation is not only expected but demanded, and there seems to be something for everyone to do. It is also a sacrificial church. Ordinary people give extraordinary amounts of money. They also sacrifice energy and time to frequent prayer meetings and community affairs. There is frequent reference to "equipping the saints for the work of ministry." Pentecostals take for granted that all their members, lay or clergy, have the same call to holiness, and they expect each of them to live the moral life. Being "overtaken by God" is only the foundational experience; the rest of the journey involves a personal moral reformation.

5) *Cultural adaptability*: An openness to unique local cultural forms in worship and prayer has contributed significantly to Pentecostalism's rapid growth. Western missionaries often confused theology with matters that pertained merely to culture. Pentecostalism's ability to sense the difference has allowed for the incorporation of forms of worship such as drums and dance that were previously rejected by mainline missionaries. I once traveled by four-wheel-drive jeep through mud and rain to join a Lutheran congregation on the slopes of Mt. Kilimanjaro in Tanzania, motivated by a desire to find some indigenous forms of

expression in the local Sunday worship. What I found were people sitting in orderly rows in pews, singing traditional German Lutheran hymns in Swahili to the tunes of a pipe organ. I've had similar experiences in Anglican Churches in Latin America and Catholic Churches in India.

EASTERN ORTHODOX AND CATHOLICS OF THE BYZANTINE TRADITION

One of the most significant blessings of the ecumenical movement is the renewal of relationship among churches of the West and East. The churches are learning to breathe again with both lungs. The gifts of the Eastern churches are many, and these few examples are but a sampling:

1) *Liturgical forms that convey a clear sense of the mystical and the transcendent*: The most common criticism of the Roman Catholic post–Vatican II liturgical reform is that it removed too many of the symbols, "smells and bells," that altered peoples' consciousness and put them in contact with something beyond their ordinary world. It seemed clear that one of the objectives behind the new translation of the Catholic sacramentary, issued in 2012 and containing all the prayers of the Mass, was to balance a sense of the immanence of God with a sense of the tremendous and fascinating mystery of God. People want their mystery! The churches of the Byzantine Tradition communicate it in the richness of their liturgical forms. We can learn from them how to strike a better balance between the *nearness* of God and the *otherness* of God.

2) *The Jesus Prayer*: A cornerstone of Eastern Christian spirituality from the founding of monasticism in the Egyptian desert, the Jesus Prayer, is entering into the blood stream of Western Christians as well. This power-packed phrase, "Lord Jesus Christ, Son of God, have mercy on me, a sinner," is aptly called the "prayer of the heart." *Lord Jesus Christ, Son of God.* As Paul says in Romans 10:9, "if you confess with your lips that Jesus is Lord and believe in your

heart that God raised him from the dead, you will be saved." Then: *Have mercy on me a sinner.* With this straightforward plea, one recognizes one's need for the Savior proclaimed in the first part of the prayer. After recognizing the need and God's saving response, there is not a great deal left to say. It remains to live, in freedom and joy, one's heartfelt gratitude. This mantric form of prayer, rooted in one's consciousness by constant repetition, is leading an increasing number of Christians from all traditions into contemplative prayer.

3) *The devotional and liturgical use of icons:* An icon does not represent a saint as divine, but as participating in the divine life, as one who has become a true icon or likeness of God. The people will kiss this image because they believe the grace of God rests upon it and in it. The Holy Spirit that filled the saints during their lives is believed to live on inexhaustibly, even after death, in their souls, in their mortal remains (hence, veneration of relics), in their writings, and in their holy images. These "windows into the infinite" communicate a spiritual reality and show us a body that perceives what usually escapes our attention: the spiritual world. Those pictured are rarely portrayed in profile, but almost always face-on so that we can converse with them and draw from them the strength and encouragement that is expressed in their serenity. Icons are a concrete expression of Eastern Christian convictions about *theosis* or divinization. Thomas à Kempis's Western classic *The Imitation of Christ* is not for them. Byzantine Christians want more than "imitation"; they want *participation* in the very life of God and believe it is our goal and destiny.

4) *A balanced role for the mother of Jesus in our devotional lives:* In Byzantine iconography, Mary never appears without her son. While almost every hymn includes her, it is always with reference to what God has done in her through the Holy Spirit. There is an admirable balance here for the consideration of Catholics who have tended at times to let her drift off into her own orbit; and Protestants who, in spite of the revered place Scripture holds for them, have

generally failed to give expression in their prayers and hymns to the biblical acclamations of Mary as "blessed are you among women" (Luke 1:42) and as one whom "all generations will call...blessed" (1:48).

5) *A place for the body in worship*: We worship not only with our mind and soul but also with our bodies. By their bending low in bows before icons, repeated signs of the cross, kissing of icons, lighting of candles, singing, kneeling, standing, the Byzantine Christians remind us to approach God with the totality of our being and to offer ourselves—body, mind, and spirit—as a "living sacrifice of praise."

ROMAN CATHOLIC

The following examples of enriching gifts to be received from Roman Catholics in the West could be predicated in large measure as well of that constituency in Anglicanism that would identify itself as Catholic, and of Eastern Christians.

1) *Deep affinity for communion with God through the Eucharist*: The Catholic Church has sometimes been referred to as "the church of the Eucharist." Its eucharistic piety finds expression in the tradition of daily Mass and devotion to the Blessed Sacrament kept in reserve as food for the sick and for the adoration of the faithful. Ironically and sadly, just at a time when a historical consensus has been achieved on the elements understood to comprise a Eucharist in the apostolic tradition,[7] and a Sunday eucharistic celebration is being reclaimed by many Protestant traditions, this rich tradition is being undermined in the Roman Catholic Church, which is adopting a communion service rite in places where there are insufficient clergy.

2) *A rich monastic tradition that witnesses to God's claim upon the totality of our lives*: "To truly seek God" is, according to the rule of St. Benedict, the very essence of monasticism. Communities of men and women who go apart to find silence to pray and to live in communion with God are

signals of transcendence in our midst. They seek in a single-minded way, as a community, ongoing growth and development in their experience of Christ's presence as the supreme and foundational reality of their lives. They remain celibate so that they can freely center their whole being and love in God and, in God, love every one of their sisters and brothers. In their "work of God" (the hours of the Divine Office), monastics have given the whole church a Prayer of Christians that, throughout the day and night, gives voice and heart to the rest of creation's praise of its Maker. There is growing evidence that this gift is being reappropriated by Protestants through their encounters with Taizé in Southern France; Grandchamp, the Protestant women's community in Areuse, Switzerland; Bose, in northern Italy; and the "new monastics" among American Evangelicals.

3) *Contemplative spirituality*: Outside the monastic tradition, contemplative spirituality received little emphasis in the life of the Christian West until the twentieth century. When the search for higher values of the Spirit emerged in the wake of World War II, reliable guides were to be found in Eastern contemplatives like Gregory of Nyssa, Origen, Dionysius, and Western contemplatives such as Richard Rolle, Julian of Norwich, Meister Eckhart, Teresa of Avila, John of the Cross, Ignatius of Loyola. In our own twentieth century, all Christians find both challenge and invitation in Evelyn Underhill's and Thomas Merton's proposal that contemplation is the goal of life for all and part of the universal call to holiness. A healthy spirituality will be able to embrace communicating with God alone and in silence as well as belting out jazzy hymns in an arena or megachurch.

4) *Religious orders and communities of apostolic life*: There is an incredible variety in the Catholic Church of apostolic religious communities of women and men (to be distinguished from monastic communities). At the foundation of each lies a distinct charism of the Holy Spirit that is incarnated in a particular apostolic work. For example, there is the

involvement of the Jesuits and the School Sisters of Notre Dame in education; the focus on home and foreign missions of the Oblate Fathers and Sisters; the efforts of the Paulists and Friars and Sisters of the Atonement in ecumenism and interfaith dialogue; and the work of the Vincentians and Sisters of Providence with the poor and the ill. These religious communities provide one of the best models for how full communion in the church might work. Each has a very different style, ethos, spirituality, and internal system of organization with its own constitution and bylaws. Diversity in piety and internal procedures of governance coexist with unity in faith and ultimate accountability to an episcopal authority in a unifying structure.

5) *Spiritual direction*: From the life of the early church onward, the tradition of spiritual direction has undergone many changes but remained a consistent practice in Catholic Christian life. This tradition offers growth in self-knowledge, discernment, the art of recognizing the movements of the Holy Spirit in one's life, an appreciation of human freedom, and it is a valuable gift for the life of members of all churches. Spiritual directors are called upon to help people make sense of their daily struggles and/or religious experiences, assisting them to cultivate, not only in prayer but in all their lived experience, an awareness of the Divine Presence. Other churches, too, are today discovering spiritual directors as a valuable resource to help searching men and women uncover the deepest treasure of their hearts, a clearer sense of purpose for their living, and the depths of faith, hope, and love with which they are already gifted.

As you can see, the exchange of spiritual gifts is like a richly laid banquet table. Offered for our spiritual nourishment are contemplative and charismatic ways of praying; *lectio divina*; the theology of icons; the tradition of spiritual direction; effective approaches to youth and young adults; the practice of annual retreats and monthly desert days; devotional practices such as praying with the psalms; methods of singing, preaching, and sharing the faith.

REJOICING IN OUR DIFFERENCES

When God puts us back together again (with the aid of our willingness to cooperate), this great Church will be marked by the dignity and reverence of the Anglicans, the order and sacraments of the Roman Catholics, the warm fellowship of the United Church, the Presbyterian desire for good preaching and the Lutheran respect for sound theology. There will be the Evangelical concern for individual salvation, the Congregational respect for the rights of the lay members, the Pentecostal reliance on the power of the Holy Spirit and the Quaker appreciation for silence. We will find there the Mennonite sense of community, the social action of the Salvation Army and the Reformed love of the Bible, all wrapped in Orthodox reverence before the mystery of God.[8]

The gift exchange is about mutual spiritual enrichment. The early Christians applied to the church the Greek word *katholike*, from which we derive the word *catholic*, which means both "universal" and "whole." It's a word that captures both the universality of the church and the wholeness or fullness of its faith and practice. One of the virtues the gift exchange calls for is humility, the recognition of the possibility that other Christians may have preserved or given richer expression to some conviction of faith or devotional practice that is either lacking or in much lower profile in our own tradition. And we see how giving fuller expression to it would enrich our own faith life and make us more truly catholic, whole.

Rev. Diane Kessler served as director of the Massachusetts Council of Churches for eighteen years. She had ample opportunity to know from personal experience how ecumenical encounters sometimes plunge us into the unfamiliar, whether in styles of worship, languages, or customs different from our own. As she relates in this story, it can at times be disorienting and challenging.

I never will forget the first time I, of staid Congregational background, experienced the charismatic fervor of African Methodist Episcopal worship. At first it was intimidating. The Holy Spirit was careening around the sanctuary in rolling waves of unbridled emotion, and I did not quite know what to do with all that passion for God. The second time I experienced this, however, I could anticipate what might be coming. This enabled me to relax into the experience. And I discovered in myself untapped emotional depths of prayer and praise to Jesus which I had not known were there. In this way, ecumenical encounters deepen and broaden our spirituality. They enhance our appreciation for the array of spiritual traditions. If we give these initially unfamiliar experiences a chance, they enrich our capacities for worship and human relationships.

Like latter-day Abrahams and Sarahs, we must be willing to venture into strange lands to encounter afresh the living God, and to jar us out of our fixed ways of being and doing. In this process we become open to new ways of seeing what God wants us to see. We must be willing to endure the uncomfortable if we are going to grow. This, in itself, is a spiritual discipline.[9]

ECUMENICAL FRIENDSHIP

During a graduate school summer, I participated in a month-long Outward Bound wilderness survival school in the lake country bordering northern Minnesota and southern Ontario.[10] Part of our instruction involved learning how to recognize various kinds of edible plants so that we could survive a period of hunger and thirst in the wild. Frequently, many forms of nourishment turned out to be things to which we lived in close proximity all our lives but had never discerned as having any particularly life-giving or life-sustaining value. Once our manner of perceiving our surrounding environment had been altered, we quickly took advantage of the gifts it offered.

Intentionally practicing receptive ecumenism is not unlike what we learned to do in the woods. It invites us to a change of perceptions and of heart toward Christians of other traditions. This, in turn, prompts us to receive from one another such gifts as liturgies, prayers, hymns, devotional practices, spiritual exercises, and approaches to the Bible. One could say that it's like learning to recognize soul food wherever it grows.

In Canterbury Cathedral in England, a number of people are honored in alcoves surrounding the main sanctuary, each one having come to holiness in a different Christian Tradition: the Russian Orthodox nun Mother Maria Skobtzova, the American Baptist pastor Martin Luther King, the Anglican Archbishop of Uganda Janani Luam, and the Polish Franciscan Fr. Maximilian Kolbe. In moments like these, we glimpse the wonderful things that God has been doing in the Communion of communions that makes up the one church of Jesus Christ throughout the world, and we discover that there is more growing in our garden than we had ever dreamed.

As we noted in the preceding chapter, receptive ecumenism calls for one to take responsibility for one's own and one's own community's learning. "Soul food" of varying kinds is growing all around us. The ecumenical movement encourages us to take a fresh look at our environment and to cultivate a taste for the many life-sustaining foods that are quietly growing there and giving nourishment to those who will take and eat.

The personal and relational are always prior to the structural and institutional. Furthermore, it is generally through our personal relationships with other Christians and becoming familiar with one another's spiritual practices that we are introduced to spiritual gifts with which we have little awareness or experience. Journeying out of our isolations; meeting, getting to know, and trusting one another; establishing friendships—these relational initiatives form the climate in which both individual Christians and separated communities become open to receiving gifts from one another. It is the climate out of which a passion for unity is born and sustained. Symbolic gestures are important among church leaders, but relationships of trust and mutual affection have to grow among members of different churches as well if receptive ecumenism is to flourish.

Friendship among people from different churches often enables improved understanding of their positions. Because friends can listen to each other sympathetically, without the presupposition of hostility or competition, they can often learn something new from each other's viewpoint. They can discover aspects of the other's position that previously they have distorted or neglected. Suddenly, they see the other's perspective in a new light.

We have to show ourselves, our churches, to one another as we are. This includes both our gifts (for growth in mutual understanding and mutual up-building in grace and love) and our limitations and failures (for pardon and healing). Reconciliation is a process in which the participants are called to a new faithfulness to the truth of Jesus Christ.

Ecumenical friendships provide a particularly intense experience of both the desire for unity and the foretaste of unity achieved. Like the disciples on the road to Emmaus, ecumenical friends walk along the road together with Christ as he opens the meaning of the scriptures to them. Because they recognize a common Lord, ecumenical friends recognize one another as his disciples and are again sustained for the long journey ahead.

Another survival technique learned from that Outward Bound program was how to treat a person for hypothermia, a condition in which the core body temperature dips to a dangerous low. We were instructed to put the person with hypothermia into a sleeping bag along with two other people who would enfold the person with their own body heat. This simple strategy has revived many a person whose vitality was visibly waning. Christians who are committed to working for unity, in spite of belonging to different churches, will do well to apply this strategy analogously in their relations with one another.

So much of the official and public ecumenical life of the churches today revolves around theological considerations that, at times, we risk forgetting the role of the personal in ecumenism. With each year of experience in church unity work, I have become more convinced that, no matter how important theological work is for reconstituting unity, the crux of the work is preserving and deepening the experience of unity on the local level. Past history proves this.

The division and separation of the churches was the result not so much of theological differences but of broken fellowship and communion. This was then confirmed by the fact that people no longer had the language to communicate with one another. Finally, they perceived each other's affirmations as mutually exclusive and thus as heresy. In the same way, theological consensus will open the door to church unity, but the only thing that will get us through that door is growing together in newly discovered fellowship and commitment.

Communities of believers, even more than articles of belief, need to be reconciled. Love alone makes truth a lived reality and sets us free to make new beginnings. One of the earliest pieces of ecumenical advice I received came during my years in seminary from a veteran Paulist ecumenist and theologian who said, "Meet people on a human level first and get to know them before you try to talk theology with them."

When we get to know one another on a human level, a trust is born that enables us together to broach the most sensitive subjects in a spirit of mutual respect. We are far more influenced by denominational attitudes in our formation than we are willing or able to admit. We have absorbed subtle prejudices toward others. We do not trust each other. And, until we can trust, we cannot hear each other. Trust is necessary if we are to "keep each other warm." The ways of keeping each other warm are as varied as the friendships and individuals concerned.

One evening, I had just returned home, still in mild shock from the death of a good friend due to a galloping cancer. I wanted in the worst way to hole up in my room, light a candle, put on some soothing music, and stare at the ceiling in easy reach of some Kleenex. Instead, I had to put on my most congenial face and stand at the door of the Catholic Basilica to greet the representatives of other churches to the 150th anniversary of the archdiocese.

When the service in the church concluded, all present were invited down the street to a hall for the reception. As I walked along with an Orthodox priest friend who was representing the Orthodox Clergy Association of the city, I shared with him the sorrow that burdened my spirit. As we entered the reception area and encountered a noisy throng with wine glasses in hand, he turned to me and said, "I don't think this fits your space. Why don't you come over to my house where it is quiet? We will open a bottle of wine and talk."

He and his wife sat at table with me in their home until one in the morning, sharing with me their painful experiences of the death of close friends and providing me with a perspective for what I was experiencing. In short, they wrapped me in their own warmth by ministering to me in a critical moment.

One of the unexpected joys of ecumenical relationships is the continual discovery of how much other Christians draw upon the same wellsprings of faith at important moments. The better we get to know one another—no matter how different our backgrounds—the more we recognize similarities between us. The Christ in me warms to the Christ in the other. Put in another way, the closer we draw to the center of our faith lives—Jesus—the closer we draw to one another.

The life of faith, personally and communally, is always, in essence, a matter of becoming more fully, more richly, what we have been called to be: the Body of Christ. So we should not be surprised that, across the whole of our lives, there is change and growth, intensification and enrichment. This is the kind of real ecumenical learning that will move us closer to finding ourselves in the other, the other in ourselves, and each in Christ.[11]

We need one another's insights and spiritual gifts to correct deficiencies and imbalances. In the ecumenical exchange, partners share as fully as possible their deepest experiences and values. The one listens and experiences and allows what comes from the other to bring forth new personal possibilities that were hitherto unrecognized and undeveloped. The Eastern Christian does not cease to be an Eastern Christian, nor does the Western Christian cease to be Western. What happens, rather, is that unsuspected possibilities, which may have lain dormant, begin to come to life in both partners as they share the rich spiritual gifts of their traditions with one another.

This approach does not undermine the confessional loyalty of the people concerned, but makes them appreciate the strength of the diverse traditions. It is a question of bearing witness together, of serving the same gospel, with the various traditions providing nourishment in the quest. Any differences in theological priorities, preoccupations, and insights will not create fear, because that is how human beings help one another to pursue the truth. Having recited the same creed, we can go on to demonstrate that the plurality of spiritual gifts enriches rather than endangers common faith.

Christ reconciled us to himself, prayed for our unity, and gave us the ministry of reconciliation. Those who undertake this work are his voice and his hands in a given time and place. Offer him yours, and he will use you.

10. FINDING SPIRITUAL COMMUNITY IN A SECULAR SOCIETY

Your local church, as they say, is not a nesting place, but merely a resting place. It's where you regularly come, like birds to the font, to refresh your drooping spirit or to draw nourishment to face the challenges ahead. It's not expected that you will stay there long, but that you will soon fly away to be about the tasks involved in cleaning the nest or providing food for those who are in it.

The language used for the church's central act of worship—Mass or *Eucharist*—offers an interesting analogy. How did that act of thanksgiving (from the Greek *eucharistia*) come to be called *Mass* in the Latin tradition? The term *Mass* is derived from the Latin word *missa* ("dismissal"), a word used in the concluding formula of Mass in Latin: "*Ite, missa est*" ("Go, it is the dismissal/the sending forth").

In Christian usage, it gradually took on a deeper meaning and expressed the missionary nature of the church: Go, you are sent forth! Sent to bring the gospel—the good news—to those on your street, in your neighborhood, and yes, to those in your office and your world of work, too. As St. Francis of Assisi said to his followers, "Preach the gospel wherever you go. If necessary, use words." And if you live it, your life will be a living word that provides its own inspiration for others.

So much of the official and public ecumenical life of the churches today revolves around theological, historical, and moral considerations that we risk forgetting the role of the personal in ecumenism. There is simply no substitute for the personal. Theological consensus will open the door to church unity, but the only thing that will get us through that door is growing together in newly discovered fellowship. It is communities of believers—even more than articles of belief—that need to be reconciled.

Church representatives have often experienced how a conversation in a bus from the airport to the hotel where a conference is being held, or chatting together during a break between sessions, can result in collaboration months later. The topic discussed may have no relationship to the conference theme, but the personal contact sets up a climate of trust that is the safety net for the whole ecumenical enterprise. What is "done" at ecumenical meetings may be effective, but it is never as critical as the relationships established in the process.

While doctrinal agreement is necessary for the expression of our unity on one level, it is obvious that such agreement is not enough. You can have it and still remain divided. A telling historical example of this is the Council of Florence (1438–45). The Greeks, in the persons of the Greek emperor, the Patriarch of Constantinople, and their theologians, met with officials and theologians from the Latin West. Beyond their desire for reunion, the Greeks sought military aid from the West against the Turks, who were nearing Constantinople. After long and painful discussions, a doctrinal agreement was worked out. All but one of the Greek bishops at the Council accepted it.

However, when the Greek bishops and theologians returned home and announced the reunion with the Latin West, the people answered with a rousing "No!" They had no love for the Latins, nor did they want to live with them in one body. Union, as worked out by ecclesiastics and theologians on the basis of doctrinal agreement, had no firm foundation in the community. Love, trust, and a desire to be of mutual service and support were lacking. The plan of reunion failed.

Similarly, in our time, we have a growing collection of joint statements and agreed statements emanating from the various national and international dialogue commissions. But they are like seeds and will be effective only if the ground has been prepared. That ground is the people in the various churches that have sponsored the process of dialogue leading to the agreed statements. If those seeds are to take root and grow, the people who make up our congregations must have opportunities to share faith and life at the local level and to come to the same conclusions as did those who officially represented them in the dialogues.

People need occasions where they can come together across denominational lines to share with each other an experience of the common Lord. Under the banner of that lordship, they will discover relationships of surprising depth. They will inevitably come to see the truth of the situation: what they share is far greater than what divides them.

In this chapter, we present an example of the ways in which a group of people in a secular society can prepare that local ground level by weaving community from below. In so doing, they make their own substantive contribution to the church's mission for unity among the followers of Jesus. They can be seasoning (salt) for one another and light for the world around them. Increasing unity in faith, life, worship, and mission among Christians will happen in much the same manner that friendship takes hold: through a gradual process of growth, not as a once and for all move. Expanding and deepening fellowship is very much to the point.

BROTHERS IN CHRIST

The story concerns a monthly gathering of community leaders in Portland, Oregon, from the private, public, and nonprofit sectors called BIC—"Brothers in Christ." BIC is an informal, monthly gathering of men in Oregon who share their stories of faith and life, and who support and encourage one another in their personal faith journeys. The group is intergenerational, racially diverse, and draws from a broad group of Catholics, Protestants, and Evangelicals.

The original group was founded by three Christian businessmen: John Castles, a retired venture capitalist and a trustee of MJ Murdock Trust; Mark Ganz, a lawyer and CEO of Cambia Health Solutions; and Don Krahmer Jr., a lawyer and shareholder in the law firm of Schwabe, Williamson & Wyatt in Portland. All three were close friends and shared a desire to build a strong community fabric rooted in faith among both Christians and those exploring their spirituality.

The first meeting had eight people, several community leaders including two lawyers, a foundation trustee, three corporate executives, an entrepreneur, a priest, and a nonprofit leader—three Catholics, two Protestants, and three Evangelicals. Initially, the target attendees were emerging professional leaders both in the business community and in the nonprofit community. There were strict rules put in place about not having the group being used for either networking or solicitation purposes. BIC was to be a group of men getting together to learn how God has entered into and is working in their lives. The group has expanded to include a number of younger twenty- to thirty-year-old professionals, several members of the clergy (Catholic, Protestant, and Evangelical), several academics including a couple of university presidents from local universities, several political leaders from both political parties, a number of nonprofit executives from faith-based and non-faith-based organizations in the region, and even a couple of individuals going through career transition or navigating personal relationship transitions.

Currently, there are three BIC groups that meet in the Portland metropolitan area. The original group, started in 2001, meets at the Arlington Club in downtown Portland and draws a diverse group of about seventy men each month from an e-mail list of about five hundred people. A second group, started in 2009, meets at the Multnomah Athletic Club in Portland and draws a group of about fifteen men each month from an e-mail list of about a hundred people. A third group, begun in 2011, meets at the Oswego Lake Country Club in Lake Oswego, Oregon, and draws about thirty-five men each month from an e-mail list of about 275.

Each group comes together for a monthly breakfast with an established format to guide the sharing at each table: quick introductions, an ice-breaker question, some sharing about one's family, and where they attend church or whether they are looking for a church community. Each month, one man from the overall group is selected well in advance to tell his personal story, including his faith journey. The last ten minutes are saved for prayer requests and for the group to pray in community prayer. Meetings run from 7:00 a.m. to 8:30 a.m.

Over the years, BIC has worked to become very diverse from a denomination, race, or age perspective. Over a third of the

Arlington Club BIC members are young men under the age of thirty-five. This group has formed a subgroup called "The Upper Room" to allow young men to gather to talk about issues affecting them in their lives. They meet for dinner and fellowship at an offsite location.

The Multnomah Athletic Club BIC was formed because of limited space at the Arlington Club and the desire to keep groups at a manageable size. Lake Oswego BIC was formed as an additional group for men in that area. BIC also encourages men to be relational with one another to help build strong local communities. BIC members in all of the groups are encouraged to be involved in their own church community and are asked not to use BIC as a substitution for belonging to their own church community.

In an interview with the founders, I asked them how this fellowship has nurtured their own faith. They all agreed that their faith has been deepened by seeing, in the stories shared, the reality of Christ showing up in their lives and the lives of the men attending the breakfasts. The preparing and sharing of personal stories have had a transformative effect on helping men pursue their journeys of faith. They witnessed to how, as followers of Christ, their desire is to encourage BIC participants to demonstrate their personal faith in the marketplace and be salt and light in the world.

They acknowledged that men do not normally share the deep details of the joys and sorrows in their lives, but are doing precisely that in their monthly sharing around the table. The key is that men are shown by example that Christ shows up through conversations with other people. Those who have strong church "homes" are strengthened in their faith by hearing the experiences shared in others' stories. Those who do not have a church congregation they call *home* are challenged to find one that fits with their denominational backgrounds and spiritual and personal needs.

BIC was not created by a larger organization. In fact, it does not even have a formal legal structure. While there are many nonprofits—both faith and non-faith based—represented at the table, the leaders have been careful not to use BIC as a means to encourage charitable work. Rather, they encourage members to cultivate deep relationship with individuals in the group outside BIC meetings, and if natural connections are made and those relationships bear fruit for the wider community, so much the better! In fact, there are numerous examples of men from BIC, motivated by convictions of faith, coming together in community service projects.

Don Krahmer effectively summed it up in saying that BIC is a community based on trusted friendship, having a servant's heart, and always having open hands toward the broader community. It is leadership based in humility and recognition that the best community in Christ is based on deep personal and trusted relationships.

"We have learned," said Don, "that trust in relationships only occurs when we are the truest we can be as human beings, including our joys, sorrows, and struggles. Sharing our personal story is the best way to connect with each other. From a founder's perspective, I think we all believe that the impact of BIC has been important, not because of what any of us have done individually or collectively, but it has come with deep prayer, reflection, and guidance from those other than ourselves. We all believe that we need to watch God show up in the human experience and notice his best work is done in community and relationship. In all we have done around BIC, we have tried to make decisions based 'in Christ' and not on personal agendas or political motivations. That is something hard to do in today's society and institutional secular organizations."

ANNUAL RETREAT

After about four years of monthly gatherings, there was a desire for members of BIC to have an opportunity to spend more time together and to get even better acquainted with one another. This took the form of an annual weekend retreat. The retreat now draws approximately 150 men. The retreat is held on the beautiful Oregon coast at the Cannon Beach Christian Conference Center.

There is a retreat speaker who gives a few talks in the course of the weekend and who is selected on a denominational, rotating basis. As "sharing your story" is an inherent part of BIC's culture, a significant amount of the retreat time is spent in small groups, allowing attendees to tell their stories and pray with one another.

I was invited to come and participate in the 2014 retreat. My encounters with other participants made it clear that while they experienced many beneficial effects, two were salient. First, they are strengthened in their faith at the retreat through the speaker's talks and the small group sessions. Second, they experience greater community connectedness both in professional and charitable circles as well as in the broader community of faith. Care is taken both to honor the different denominational traditions, as well as to provide a forum where individuals share their stories and where Christ has and is showing up for them.

One of the men, Kevin, witnessed to this.

> BIC has provided the best opportunity in my life to journey together, over the long haul, with brothers from the Catholic tradition. Being the son of a well-known evangelist, and now serving as the president of an organization that works to unite churches across the denominational spectrum to both love and serve the community as well as share the good news, I grew up with a greater than average awareness of and appreciation for the beauty of the diversity within the Body of Christ.
>
> Having said that, my experience had predominantly been within the evangelical and, to a lesser extent, the mainline Protestant traditions. I lived for eight years in Latin America as a kid and had no negative attitudes towards Catholics but also had hardly any direct, meaningful relationships with them.
>
> BIC has become a huge blessing to me for many reasons, not least of which is the rich depth of relationships with my Catholic brothers. By focusing exclusively on what we have in common, it's served to help affirm our common ground in Christ.
>
> Hearing both Evangelical and Catholic brothers share the stories of their Christian journey, always including family history and a sense of spiritual history, has forever changed my sense of what unity among Christians can be like.
>
> For many it's been the first time they've consistently heard "testimonies" from the evangelical perspective that reference the formative role of regular time spent in the study of the scriptures and a clear point of "committing

one's life to Christ," often in childhood, but for others as an adult.

For some, BIC has been the first time they've publically shared what Christ means to them, in the company of respected peers. For others, it's clearly been an eye opener to see that our Catholic brothers share a love of Scripture, amplified by church tradition, and that a living, personal relationship with Christ exists in all of us.

Listening to Fr. Rick Ganz (a longtime BIC member, a Jesuit priest, and brother of BIC co-founder Mark Ganz), in particular, has always been a blessing. He's been the first priest that I've had the privilege of knowing more deeply, and his perspectives have drawn me closer to Christ.

BIC has given all of us strength and a sense of solidarity that's vital in a 'non-Bible belt' place like Portland, Oregon, where all followers of Christ taken together would still constitute a minority, at least if measured in any meaningful way, for example, church attendance.

What I love about BIC is that the unity isn't around political or social issues, important as those may be, but around telling our stories and encouraging each other to grow in our faith. My neighbor across the street, Brad, who grew up Catholic but by his own admission "didn't really get it," came to a clear faith in Christ at the BIC retreat two years ago. He's been equally influenced and encouraged by both the Evangelical and Catholic "sides," so to speak, and it's been a blessing to see him now reading (or listening on his iPad) to the Bible nearly every day, asking me questions, even sharing how God has been changing his life with others.

One of the unexpected joys of ecumenical relationships is the constant discovery of how much other Christians draw upon the same wellsprings of faith at important moments in their lives. The better we get to know one another, the more we recognize similarities between us. The Christ in me warms to the Christ in the other. And the closer we draw to the center of our faith lives, the closer we draw to each other.

Another of the retreat participants, Joey, shared how his experience in the BIC breakfasts and retreats has helped him see that the Lord and his Holy Spirit are present and active in life-giving ways in Christian denominations as well as in his own nondenominational congregation.

> It has been a huge blessing to worship and pray with believers of many different denominations in our BIC gatherings. My life has been enriched by Catholics, Lutherans, Baptists, and so many others that I do not typically get to have fellowship with. I have been prayed for and encouraged by strong men of faith from many different traditional backgrounds.
>
> On Friday night around the campfire, as our retreat director was guiding us to a place of quietness and surrender to our Lord Jesus Christ, I looked around and saw so many faces of men from different traditions of Christian faith, all coming together to bow down and worship the same God and King. It was as if all the peripheral differences fade away as we focus on the true heart of the Christian faith, Jesus Christ.
>
> Many of my friends consistently think and speak about how Catholics have no personal relationship with Jesus. They believe that most or all Catholics simply follow traditions for the sake of traditions and that God is a distant entity of non-relationship to them. This is a drastically different perception from the reality of what I see in the Catholic men associated with BIC. At BIC, I see Catholic men who very much have a deep and life-altering relationship with Jesus Christ; men who hold him as best friend, Father, and King.
>
> I had a number of faith challenges at an early age that helped form and develop my relationship with God in a very real and personal way. These challenges forced me to question my faith in a way that led me into a deeper relationship with God than I ever thought possible. They

helped me to see which differences in our faith touch core
beliefs and which ones do not. Jesuit High School played
a huge role in my faith formation and helped make my
faith my own. Even though I am still associated with a nondenominational Christian faith, the Catholic Church has
been a huge blessing to me.

Another retreatant, Ben, paid tribute to the role of leadership
in the creation of a network such as BIC. "The unity reflected within
BIC," said Ben, "is all about leadership and how Don Krahmer represents the 'person of peace' who sets the tone as the intermediary
and connector. Any ecumenism that exists does so because Don
models it and builds it. Don's leadership cannot be understated."

Ben related how, when BIC started, it was originally a consciously chosen group of men who represented leaders whom others
aspired to be with. That original group was intentionally mixed with
Catholics and Protestants, but denominational affiliation was never
a barrier because there was simply too much respect in the room. The
men connected as leaders and peers first and articulated their religious affiliation second. The focus is on taking new members where
they are in their faith walks, not in trying to convince or persuade
them that one way of thinking is better than another. Consistent
with this, any discussions of divisive political issues are not allowed
in BIC.

"Don has been very intentional," said Ben, "about keeping a
steady flow of new members coming into the group that has been
formed and continues to grow, all the while keeping it on stream
with its objectives. He is also very intentional and discerning in
helping weave the community that has been formed and continues
to grow."

Ben indicated that while one doesn't attend BIC unless one is
invited, there is no attendance requirement. Some folks may attend
a couple of times a year and others are there on a monthly basis.

There is a generous invitation policy developing. This
means that younger and more diverse leaders are attending. While this also leads to some of the leaders potentially not being chief executives or presidents, it is also

challenging the perception that BIC is only for "insiders." Don certainly has a small group of leaders he vets decisions with. The ethos is likely discussed, and the implications for growth have been approved by those vested in the long-term outcomes emerging. If I were to distill my thoughts into two sentences, they would be: Ecumenism and unity emerges when leadership is intentional and there is a creative unifying idea. In the case of BIC, the unifying idea is leadership connection for our community.

To say as much is to recognize that, while Christian unity was not the primary motivating reason for founding BIC, it has been an active agent in creating relationships of admiration and respect among members of different churches. And those relationships have deepened faith in all directions, oftentimes resulting in joint projects of social service and thereby providing a positive witness of the followers of Jesus honoring him by keeping his new commandment to "love one another as I have loved you."

The strength of BIC is that each member is respected no matter what denominational soil he is rooted in. This acceptance fosters communication, which in turn leads to a greater understanding of each other. And from this, the members witness to how Christ shows himself to us—many times unexpectedly—through others.

A further effect that occurs is better understanding between and among denominations by creating relationships of deep trust among BIC members through the shared experience. A fruit of this is a more respectful and focused discussion of individual denominational beliefs as well as a clarification of one's own beliefs.

An association such as BIC makes a precious and significant contribution to the unity of Christ's followers and their witness to the world. We need new ways of inviting people to share life and faith, new social networks that enable people to "be there" for one another in prayer and service. In so doing, we will be building up the Body of Christ from below, from the ground level. With the living stones of our lives, a spiritual house is being built.

In 2013, a group of women in contact with some BIC leaders launched a similar group for women called SIS—Sisters in the Spirit. The SIS group now meets monthly at the Multnomah Athletic Club and draws approximately sixty women from diverse backgrounds as does BIC. A notably strong emphasis has been placed on intergenerational, denominational, and racial diversity in the group's membership and the focus, as in BIC, is on providing a safe forum for sharing individual personal and faith stories. In other words, the seeds sown by BIC's witness are taking root under the life-giving influence of the Holy Spirit and are already growing in new ways and places.

May the story of BIC and SIS serve as an invitation to both men and women in secular civic communities far and near to ask themselves, What could we do *here*?

CONCLUSION

The quest to realize and give expression to unity among Christians should be for us all an essential spiritual practice in our life of faith. It has two fundamental assumptions. First, Christian unity is an intrinsic part of the transformed life God gives us in following Jesus. And second, it is a goal yet to be fully realized in concrete, visible, human terms.[1]

Over the past forty years, the progress toward agreement in faith through theological dialogue has been substantial, but the time has come for us to give it more tangible expression on the grassroots level, both individually and congregationally, to look one another in the eye with both love and esteem and acknowledge what we see to be truly of Christ and of the gospel. The mission given us by Christ obliges and compels us to engage more deeply and widely in a partnership of mission, coupled with common witness and joint prayer.[2]

Thy will be done are words contained in the only prayer that Jesus taught us. These words in the Our Father are prayed every day by countless believers from all churches. In John's Gospel, Jesus revealed his will for the church when he prayed to the Father that all of his disciples be one so that the world may believe (see John 17:21). To pray that the Lord's will be done necessarily requires a wholehearted endeavor on our part to embrace his will for and gift of unity.[3]

In this book, we have reflected on the contribution each of us can make to that unity—in our parishes and social action networks, as interchurch couples or members of monastic and religious communities and lay movements, as students or professors, and as an association of community leaders from the private, public, and nonprofit sectors. Each of us *can* make a difference!

At the same time, we all recognize that the unity of the one Church of Christ transcends human powers and gifts. Thus do we place our hope in the prayer of Christ for the church, in the love of the Father for us, and in the power of the Holy Spirit, knowing that "hope does not disappoint us, because God's love has been poured into our hearts through the Holy Spirit that has been given to us" (Rom 5:5) (Decree on Ecumenism 24). Could there be, then, a more appropriate way for us to close than with a prayer?

> O God, holy and eternal Trinity,
> we pray for your church in the world.
> Sanctify its life; renew its worship;
> empower its witness; heal its divisions.
> make visible its unity.
>
> Lead us, with all our brothers and sisters
> towards communion
> in faith, life, and witness,
> so that, united in the one body
> by the one Spirit,
> we may together witness
> to the perfect unity of your love.[4]

NOTES

INTRODUCTION

1. Thomas Ryan, *Disciplines for Christian Living: Interfaith Perspectives* (New York/Mahwah, NJ: Paulist Press, 1993); *Prayer of Heart and Body: Meditation and Yoga as Christian Spiritual Practice* (New York/Mahwah, NJ: Paulist Press, 1995); *The Sacred Art of Fasting: Preparing to Practice* (Woodstock, VT: SkyLight Paths, 2005); *Interreligious Prayer: A Christian Guide* (New York/Mahwah, NJ: Paulist Press, 2008).

CHAPTER 1

1. Ron Rolheiser, "Jesus Calls Us to Greater Concern for Christian Unity," *Western Catholic Reporter*, February 25, 2013, 16.

2. Steven Harmon, *Ecumenism Means You, Too* (Eugene, OR: Cascade Books, 2010), 84.

3. Pontifical Council for Promoting Christian Unity, *Directory for the Application of Principles and Norms on Ecumenism* (Vatican City: Vatican Press, 1993), http://www.vatican.va/roman_curia/pontifical_councils/chrstuni/general-docs/rc_pc_chrstuni_doc_19930325_directory_en.html.

4. *Breaking Barriers, Nairobi 1975: Official Report, Fifth Assembly, World Council of Churches*, ed. David M. Paton (London: SPCK, 1976), 317, 318.

5. William Temple, "Sermon at the Opening Service," in *The Ecumenical Movement: An Anthology of Key Texts and Voices*, ed. Michael Kinnamon and Brian Cope (Grand Rapids, MI: Eerdmans, 1997), 8, 19.

6. See the Decree on Ecumenism (*Unitatis Redintegratio*) in *Vatican Council II: The Conciliar and Post Conciliar Documents*, ed. Austin Flannery, OP (Collegeville, MN: Liturgical Press, 1975), http://www.vatican.va/archive/hist_councils/ii_vatican_council/documents/vat-ii_decree_196 41121_unitatis-redintegratio_en.html.

7. World Council of Churches, *The Church: Towards a Common Vision* (Geneva: WCC Publications, 2013), nos. 1, 13, http://www.oikou

mene.org/en/resources/documents/wcc-commissions/faith-and-order-com
mission/i-unity-the-church-and-its-mission/the-church-towards-a-com
mon-vision.

8. Paul Avis, *Reshaping Ecumenical Theology* (New York: Continuum, 2010), 190, 194.

9. Pope John Paul II, "*Ut Unum Sint*: On Commitment to Ecumenism," *Origins* 25 (June 8, 1995): 50–72.

10. Edward Idris Cardinal Cassidy, "Vatican II and Catholic Principles of Ecumenism," *Bulletin/Centro Pro Unione* 54 (Fall 1996): 7.

11. Bishop Kallistos of Diokleia, "Orthodoxy and the Eastern Catholics: Problem or Opportunity?" *Eastern Churches Journal* 9, no. 2 (Summer 2002): 20–22.

12. John Paul II, "*Ut Unum Sint*," 49–72, no. 9.

13. Ronald Roberson, "Remembering Antioch: The Maronite Catholic Church and the Ecumenical Movement" (talk given, Brooklyn, NY, July 11, 2003).

14. Avis, *Reshaping*, 36–38.

15. Homily of Pope Francis, Catholic Cathedral of the Holy Spirit, Istanbul, November 29, 2014.

16. Carl E. Braaten and Robert W. Jensen, eds., *In One Body through the Cross: The Princeton Proposal for Christian Unity* (Grand Rapids, MI: Eerdmans, 2003), nos. 10b, 19, 44.

17. Cardinal Kurt Koch, "Fundamental Aspects of Ecumenism and Future Perspectives" (talk given, The Catholic University of America, Washington, DC, November 3, 2011), http://www.katolsk.no/tro/tema/eku menikk/artikler/developments-and-challenges-in-ecumenism-today.

18. Cardinal Edward Idris Cassidy as quoted by Cardinal K Koch in "Developments and Challenges in Ecumenism Today" (address, Trondheim, Norway, July 29, 2011), http://www.katolsk.no/tro/tema/ekumenikk/artikler /developments-and-challenges-in-ecumenism-today.

19. Avis, *Reshaping*, 34.

20. Cindy Wooden, "Desire for Christian Unity Is Widespread and Strong: Pope," The Prairie Messenger, November 19, 2014.

21. Canadian Conference of Catholic Bishops, "A Church in Dialogue: Towards the Restoration of Unity Among Christians, Celebrating the 50th Anniversary of the Second Vatican Council's Decree on Ecumenism, *Unitatis Redintegratio*, 1964–2014," 18. http://www.cccb.ca/site/ images/stories/pdf/A_Church_in_Dialogue_long_version_EN.PDF.

22. "A Church in Dialogue," 23.

23. "A Church in Dialogue," 9.

CHAPTER 2

1. Koch, "Fundamental Aspects of Ecumenism" (see chap. 1, n. 17).

2. Thomas P. Rausch, "Where is Ecumenism Today?" *Ecumenical Trends* 42, no. 2 (February 2013): 28.

3. Michael Kinnamon and Brian E. Cope, eds., general introduction to *The Ecumenical Movement: An Anthology of Key Texts and Voices* (Grand Rapids, MI: Eerdmans, 1997), 1.

4. Jeffrey Gros, "Unity Is on the Way: US Churches are Moving towards a Jubilee," *One World* 210 (November 1995): 6, 7.

5. Kinnamon and Cope, *Ecumenical Movement*, 2, 3.

6. "Report on the Section on Unity," in *The New Delhi Report: The Third Assembly of the World Council of Churches, 1961* (New York: Association, 1962), 116.

7. See http://www.vatican.va/archive/hist_councils/ii_vatican_council/documents/vat-ii_decree_19641121_unitatis-redintegratio_en.html.

8. "The Unity of the Church: Gift and Calling—The Canberra Statement," quoted in Kinnamon and Cope, *Ecumenical Movement*, 124.

9. Ibid.

10. Avis, *Reshaping Ecumenical Theology*, 150 (see chap. 1, n. 8).

11. Enzo Bianchi, "A Spirituality of Communion: Unity in Diversity," in *Searching for Christian Unity*, ed. Walter Kasper (Hyde Park, NY: New City Press, 2007), 205.

12. Lorelei F. Fuchs, "The Holy Spirit and the Development of *Communio/Koinonia* Ecclesiology as a Fundamental Paradigm for Ecumenical Engagement," in *The Holy Spirit, The Church, and Christian Unity* (Leuven, Belgium: University Press, 2005), 166–71.

13. Walter Kasper, *That They May All Be One* (New York: Burns and Oates, 2004), 50.

14. Agreed Statement of the Tenth Round of the U.S. Lutheran–Roman Catholic Dialogue, in *The Church as Koinonia of Salvation: Its Structure and Ministries*, ed. Randall Lee and Jeffrey Gros (Washington, DC: U.S. Conference of Catholic Bishops, 2005), 5–145.

15. Kasper, *That They May All Be One*, 58.

16. World Council of Churches, *The Church*, viii, ix (see chap. 1, n. 7).

17. World Council of Churches, "Baptism, Eucharist, and Ministry," Faith and Order Paper no. 111 (Geneva: WCC Publications, 1982), http://www.oikoumene.org/en/resources/documents/wcc-commissions/faith-and-order-commission/i-unity-the-church-and-its-mission/baptism-eucharist-and-ministry-faith-and-order-paper-no-111-the-lima-text.

18. World Council of Churches, *The Church*, 10.

19. Ibid., viii, ix.

20. Ibid., 1, 2.

21. Koch, "Fundamental Aspects of Ecumenism." The citation of Pope Benedict XVI is from his vesper homily at the conclusion of the Week of Prayer for Christian Unity in the Basilica St. Paul Outside the Walls, January 25, 2011.

22. Avis, *Reshaping Ecumenical Theology*, 200.

23. Pontifical Council for Promoting Christian Unity, *Directory for the Application*, no. 16, 20 (see chap. 1, n. 3).

24. World Council of Churches, *The Church*, 16.

25. Bianchi, "A Spirituality of Communion," 209.

26. "Christian Understanding of Unity in an Age of Radical Diversity," a Gathering Draft for the 2010 Centennial Ecumenical Gathering and General Assembly of the National Council of Churches of Christ in the USA and Church World Service, New Orleans, LA, October 30, 2010.

27. Leonard Hodgson, ed., *The Second World Conference on Faith and Order held at Edinburgh, August 3–18, 1937* (New York: MacMillan, 1938), 59–60.

28. Ola Tjorhom, *Visible Church—Visible Unity* (Collegeville, MN: Liturgical Press, 2004), 88.

29. "Christian Understanding of Unity," 2.

30. "Christian Understanding of Unity," 4, 5.

31. Homily of Pope Francis, Catholic Cathedral of the Holy Spirit, Istanbul, Turkey, November 29, 2014, http://w2.vatican.va/content/francesco/en/homilies/2014/documents/papa-francesco_20141129_omelia-turchia.html.

32. Tjorhom, *Visible Church*, 88, 89.

33. Avis, *Reshaping Ecumenical Theology*, 32.

34. Koch, "Fundamental Aspects of Ecumenism."

35. Michael Root, "The Ecumenical Futures: Discerning the Signs of the Times" (presentation, International Ecumenical Seminar of the Institute for Ecumenical Research, Strasbourg, France, July 1994).

36. Tjorhom, *Visible Church*, 92, 93.

37. Avis, *Reshaping Ecumenical Theology*, 44.

38. Pontifical Council for Promoting Christian Unity, *Directory for the Application*, no. 13.

39. John Paul II, "*Ut Unum Sint*," no. 55, 62 (see chap. 1, n. 9).

40. See http://www.globalchristianforum.org/gatherings.html.

41. Cardinal Walter Kasper, "Foreword," in *Celebrating a Century of Ecumenism*, ed. John Radano (Grand Rapids, MI: Eerdmans, 2012), ix, x.

42. Kasper, *That They May All Be One*, 71, 72.

43. Ibid., 72, 73.

CHAPTER 3

1. Pontifical Council for Promoting Christian Unity, *Directory for the Application*, no. 22 (see chap. 1, n. 3).

2. Ibid., no. 55.

3. Pontifical Council for Promoting Christian Unity, "The Ecumenical Dimension of the Formation of Those Engaged in Pastoral Work," March 9, 1998, no. 2, http://www.vatican.va/roman_curia/pontifical _councils/chrstuni/general-docs/rc_pc_chrstuni_doc_19950316_ecumeni cal-dimension_en.html.

4. John Paul II, *Ut Unum Sint* (On Commitment to Ecumenism), May 25, 1995, http://www.vatican.va/holy_father/john_paul_ii/encyclicals /documents/hf_jp-ii_enc_25051995_ut-unum-sint_en.html.

5. Gary B. Reierson, "Ecumenism from 'The Bottom Up,'" *Ecumenical Trends* 31 (March 2002): 43.

6. Cardinal Walter Kasper, *Harvesting the Fruits: Basic Aspects of Christian Faith in Ecumenical Dialogue* (New York, Continuum: 2009).

7. Jeffrey Gros and Daniel S. Mulhall, eds., *The Ecumenical Christian Dialogues and the Catechism of the Catholic Church* (Mahwah, NJ: Paulist Press, 2006).

8. Kinnamon and Cope, "The Lund Statement," in *Ecumenical Movement*, 462, 463 (see chap. 2, n. 3).

9. Diane Kessler, ed., *Receive One Another: Hospitality in Ecumenical Perspective* (Geneva, Switzerland: WCC Publications, 2005), 43, 44.

10. Kessler, *Receive One Another*, 45.

11. Kessler, *Receive One Another*, 45, 46.

12. Thomas Ryan, "Parish Ecumenical Representatives," *Ecumenism* 149 (March 2003): 33, 34.

13. Pontifical Council for Promoting Christian Unity, *Directory for the Application*, no. 67.

14. List compiled both from my own experience and various sources, with special reference to *Local Ecumenism and Interfaith Cooperation* (Garrison, NY: Graymoor Ecumenical Institute, 1985).

15. Ryan, *Interreligious Prayer*.

CHAPTER 4

1. Association of Interchurch Families Press Release, June 27–29, 2008, National Conference, Louisville, KY.

2. George Kilcourse, *Double Belonging: Interchurch Families and Christian Unity* (New York: Paulist Press, 1992).

3. Second World Gathering of Interchurch Families, "Interchurch Families and Christian Unity: Rome 2003," 2, 3, http://interchurchfamilies.org/confer/rome2003/documents/roma2003_en.pdf.

4. Second World Gathering of Interchurch Families, "Interchurch Families," 4.

5. Ibid.

6. Pontifical Council for Promoting Christian Unity, *Directory for the Application*, no. 66 (see chap 1, n. 3).

7. Pope John Paul II, *The Pope in Britain: Collected Homilies and Speeches* (Slough, UK: St. Paul Publications, 1982), 30.

8. Pope Benedict XVI, "Address of the Holy Father: Ecumenical Encounter," Warsaw, Poland, May 25, 2006, http://www.vatican.va/holy_father/benedict_xvi/speeches/2006/may/documents/hf_ben-xvi_spe_20060525_incontro-ecumenico_en.html.

9. For more information see http://www.dur.ac.uk/theology.religion/ccs/projects/receptiveecumenism/.

10. See http://interchurchfamilies.org/journal/journal_index.html. While the *Interchurch Families* journal is published by the Association of Interchurch Families in England, it is intended to serve the needs of English-speaking families internationally. The entire journal has since been published online.

11. United States Conference of Catholic Bishops, "Non-Catholics and Holy Communion," http://www.usccb.org/prayer-and-worship/the-mass/order-of-mass/liturgy-of-the-eucharist/guidelines-for-the-reception-of-communion.cfm.

12. M. G. Lawler and T. A. Salzman, "A Pastoral Letter of the United States Catholic Bishops on Marriage: A Commentary," *INTAMS Review* 15, no. 2 (Fall 2009): 219.

13. U.S. Religious Knowledge Survey (The Pew Forum on Religion and Public Life, September 28, 2010), http://pewforum.org/U-S-Religious-Knowledge-Survey-Who-Knows-What-About-Religion.aspx#Christianity.

14. Though this reflects well the experience of interchurch families, ecclesiologically, it is a difficult term. No person can belong twice to the Body of Christ, the church. The French use the term *double insertion*, referring to being inserted into the Body of Christ, the church, through two different traditions. That may prove to be a better term.

15. Resources for couples in this situation can be found at www.interchurchfamilies.org and especially in the "Sacramental Resources" found there.

16. Fr. John Coventry, "Getting Married," *Interchurch Families* 6 (January 1982, rev. 1992), http://interchurchfamilies.org/resource/marriage /getting_married.pdf.

17. Taken from a pamphlet distributed by the AAIF, titled "What is life like if you and your family share your Christian faith within two different Church traditions? And what can your church families do to make a difference?"

18. "Beatitudes for Interchurch Families," *Journal of the Association of Interchurch Families* 6, no. 1 (January 1998): 1.

CHAPTER 5

1. Pontifical Council for Promoting Christian Unity, *Directory for the Application*, no. 138 (see chap 1, n. 3).

2. Ibid.

3. Paul Robichaud, CSP, and Thomas Ryan, CSP, "From Conversion to Dialogue: The Transformation of Paulist Mission following Vatican II," *Ecumenical Trends* 38, no. 3 (March 2009): 42.

4. Ibid.

5. John O'Malley, *What Happened at Vatican II* (Cambridge, MA: Harvard University Press, 2008), 290–319.

6. Daniel Tobin, "A New Digital Initiative in Catholic-Evangelical Relations," *Koinonia* (Fall 2012): 46, http://www.paulist.org/ecumenism/ new-digital-world-initiative-catholic-evangelical-relations.

7. Thomas Ryan, CSP, "100 Years of Prayer for Christian Unity," *Western Catholic Reporter*, January 14, 2008, 13.

8. Enzo Bianchi, *Monastic Life and the Ecumenical Dialogue* (Monastery of Bose, 2001).

9. Bianchi, *Monastic Life*, 19.

10. J. L. G. Balada, *The Story of Taizé* (London: Mowbray, 1980), 36.

11. Meditations by Brother Roger in *Taizé: Opening Paths of Trust* (Taizé Press, 2003), 29–32.

12. Olivier Clement, *Taizé: A Meaning to Life* (Chicago: GIA Publications, 1997), 71.

13. Four Proposals for "seeking visible communion among all who love Christ," http://www.taize.fr/en_article16219.html.

14. Grandchamp, "Today," http://www.grandchamp.org/pages/en/ today.html.

15. Sr. Françoise, "Grandchamp: A Contemplative Community," *Ecumenism* 98 (June 1990): 29.

16. "The Community in Brief," http://www.monasterodibose.it/en/community/presentation.

17. Bianchi, *Monastic Life*, 20.

18. Molly Worthen, "The Unexpected Monks," *Boston Globe*, February 3, 2008, http://www.prayerfoundation.org/dailyoffice/y_boston _globe_the_unexpected_monks.htm.

19. Ibid.

20. Rob Moll, "The New Monasticism," *Christianity Today* 49, no. 9 (September 2005): 40, http://www.christianitytoday.com/ct/2005/september /16.38.html?start=1.

21. Ibid., 40, 41.

22. Rutba House, *Schools for Conversion: 12 Marks of a New Monasticism* (Eugene, OR: Cascade Press, 2005).

23. Moll, "The New Monasticism," 46.

24. See http://www.together4europe.org/en/press-en/dossier/280-maria-voce-presentation-of-together-for-europe/file.html. For more info see www.together4europe.org.

25. Information and Reflection by Cardinal Walter Kasper, November 23, 2007, at the Meeting of the Holy Father with the College of Cardinals at the Vigil of the public Ordinary Consistory.

26. Chiara Lubich, *The Secret of Unity* (London: New City, 1997), 21, 22.

27. Peter Parmense, "Focolare and Ecumenism: Dialogue of Life," *Ecumenical Trends* 35, no. 2 (February 2006): 15.

28. Ibid.

29. Focolare, http://www.focolare.org/usa/en/about-us/in-brief/.

30. Syndesmos, http://syndesmostemporary.blogspot.com/p/constitu tion-of-syndemsos.html.

31. Sant'Egidio, http://www.santegidio.org/pageID/4/langID/en/ECU MENISM_AND_DIALOGUE.html.

32. Michael Byrnes, "The Sword of the Spirit," *Ecumenism* 98 (June 1990): 7.

33. Sword of the Spirit, http://www.swordofthespirit.net/aboutus. html.

34. Byrnes, "The Sword of the Spirit," 8.

35. L'Arche USA, http://www.larcheusa.org/who-we-are/identity-and-mission/.

36. International Council of L'Arche, *Ecumenism in l'Arche 2* (Noyon, France: International Council of L'Arche, 1994), 33–55.

37. Margaret O'Donnell, "L'Arche: After 25 years," *Ecumenism* 98 (June 1990).

38. Robert S. Bilheimer, *Breakthrough: The Emergence of the Ecumenical Tradition* (Grand Rapids, MI: Eerdmans, 1989), 217, 221.

39. Ibid., 221–23.

CHAPTER 6

1. Libertus Hodemaker, "Church and World," in *Dictionary of the Ecumenical Movement*, ed. Nicolas Lossky et al. (Geneva: WCC Publications, 2002), 190.

2. Hodemaker, "Church and World," 191, 192.

3. "Encyclicals," http://www.catholicsocialteaching.org.uk/resources/documents/.

4. Ibid.

5. Pope Francis, *Evangelii Gaudium*, The Joy of the Gospel, http://w2.vatican.va/content/francesco/en/apost_exhortations/documents/papa-francesco_esortazione-ap_20131124_evangelii-gaudium.html.

6. Paul Albrecht, "Life and Work," in *Dictionary of the Ecumenical Movement*, ed. Nicolas Lossky et al. (Geneva: WCC Publications, 2002), 691.

7. Ibid.

8. Ibid., 692.

9. D. Preman Niles, "Justice, Peace and the Integrity of Creation," in *Dictionary of the Ecumenical Movement*, ed. Nicolas Lossky et al. (Geneva: WCC Publications, 2002), 631.

10. Ibid., 632.

11. Ibid.

12. Jonathan Luxmoore, "Churches Unite, Target Climate Change," *Western Catholic Reporter*, December 10, 2013, 10.

13. Luxmoore, "Churches Unite," 10.

14. See http://en.radiovaticana.va/news/2015/06/18/metropolitan_john_zizioulas_laudato_si_give_orthodox_grea/1152356.

15. Michael Kinnamon, *Can a Renewal Movement Be Renewed? Questions for the Future of Ecumenism* (Grand Rapids, MI: Eerdmans, 2014), 140.

16. World Council of Churches, "Called to be the One Church" (as adopted), http://www.oikoumene.org/en/resources/documents/assembly/2006-porto-alegre/1-statements-documents-adopted/christian-unity-and-message-to-the-churches/called-to-be-the-one-church-as-adopted.

17. World Council of Churches, "Church and World: The Unity of the Church and the Renewal of Human Community," http://www.oikoumene.org/en/resources/documents/wcc-commissions/faith-and-order-commission/vi-church-and-world/church-and-world.

18. Hodemaker, "Church and World," 193.

19. Kinnamon, *Can a Renewal Movement Be Renewed?* 64.

20. Annandale Christian Community for Action, http://www.accacares.org.

21. ACCA, "ACCA—More than Forty Five Years of Community Action for the Poor," http://www.accacares.org/history.html.

22. Canadian Conference of Catholic Bishops, "A Church in Dialogue," 22 (see chap. 1, n. 21).

CHAPTER 7

1. Mitzi J. Budde, "The Vocation for Unity in Theological Education," in *Staying One, Remaining Open*, ed. J. Barney Hawkins IV and Richard J. Jones (New York: Church Publishing, 2010), 91.

2. Joint Working Group between the Roman Catholic Church and the World Council of Churches, "Ecumenical Formation: Ecumenical Reflections and Suggestions," *The Ecumenical Review* 45, no. 4 (1993): no. 9, 492.

3. Oliver S. Tomkins, ed. *The Third World Conference on Faith and Order, Lund 1952* (London: SCM, 1953), 15–16.

4. Pontifical Council for Promoting Christian Unity, *Directory for the Application*, no. 55, 58 (see chap. 1, n. 3).

5. Konrad Raiser, "Fifty Years of Ecumenical Formation: Where Are We? Where Are We Going?" *The Ecumenical Review* 48, no. 4 (1996): 440.

6. Julio de Santa Ana, "Research and Ecumenical Formation," *The Ecumenical Review* 48, no. 4 (1996): 503.

7. Joan Delaney, "Ecumenical Formation in the 1990s and Beyond," *The Ecumenical Review* 48, no. 1 (1996): 7.

8. Joint Working Group, "Ecumenical Formation," no. 17, 493.

9. Ibid., no. 20, 493.

10. Pontifical Council for Promoting Christian Unity, *Directory for the Application*, no. 65.

11. Raiser, "Fifty Years," 447.

12. Pontifical Council for Promoting Christian Unity, *Directory for the Application*, no. 89e.

13. Raiser, "Fifty Years," 449.

14. John B. Lindner and Linda-Marie Deloff, "The U.S. Bossey Assessment Project," *The Ecumenical Review* 48, no. 4 (1996): 464, 465.

15. The term *Oriental Orthodox Churches* is now generally used to describe a group of six ancient Eastern Churches: the Armenian Apostolic Church, the Coptic Orthodox Church, the Ethiopian Orthodox Church, the Syrian Orthodox Church, the Malankara Orthodox Syrian Church,

and the Eritrean Orthodox Church. Although they are in communion with one another, each is fully independent and possesses many distinctive traditions.

16. Thomas Ryan, *Tales of Christian Unity: The Adventures of an Ecumenical Pilgrim* (New York/Mahwah, NJ: Paulist Press, 1984).

17. Thomas Ryan, *A Survival Guide for Ecumenically Minded Christians* (Ottawa, ON: Novalis, 1989).

18. Daniel Martensen, "Introduction," in *The Teaching of Ecumenics*, ed. Samuel Amirtham and Cyris H.S. Moon (Geneva: WCC Publications, 1987), xii.

19. Lutheran-Roman Catholic Conversations, "Ways to Community," in *Growth in Agreement*, ed. Harding Meyer and Lucas Vischer (Geneva: WCC Publications, 1984), 230.

20. Anglican-Methodist Dialogue, "Sharing in the Apostolic Communion," in *Growth in Agreement II*, ed. Jeffrey Gros, Harding Meyer, and William G. Rusch (Geneva: WCC Publications, 2000), 59.

21. Mitzi J. Budde, "The Vocation for Unity in Theological Education," in *Staying One, Remaining Open*, ed. J. Barney Hawkins IV and Richard J. Jones (New York: Church Publishing, 2010), 98.

22. Ibid., 102.

23. Ibid., 90, 91.

24. Pontifical Council for Promoting Christian Unity, *Directory for the Application*, no. 79, 80, 88, 91.

25. Pontifical Council for Promoting Christian Unity, "The Ecumenical Dimension" (see chap. 3, n. 3).

26. Joint Working Group, "Ecumenical Formation," no. 11, 492.

27. Ecumenical Institute at the Château de Bossey, "Study at Bossey," http://institute.oikoumene.org/en/study-at-bossey.

28. Centro Pro Union, "Summer Course," http://www.prounione.urbe.it/new/eng/summercourse.html.

29. Graduate Theological Foundation, http://www.gtfeducation.org.

30. CADEIO, http://cadeio.org.

31. See http://www.strasbourginstitute.org/en/summer-seminar/.

32. Prairie Center for Ecumenism, "Program Overview," http://pcecumenism.ca/content/program-overview.

33. Kipley Lukan Yaworski, "Ecumenical Formation Program Launched," *The Prairie Messenger*, September 10, 2014, 4.

34. Ibid.

35. Pontifical Council for Promoting Christian Unity, "The Ecumenical Dimension."

36. Canadian Conference of Catholic Bishops, "A Church in Dialogue," 24 (see chap. 1, n. 21).

37. Pontifical Council for Promoting Christian Unity, *Directory for the Application*, no. 83.

38. Ibid., no. 90

39. Ibid., no. 93.

40. Ibid., no. 67.

41. Ibid., no. 68.

42. Ibid., no. 66.

43. John S. Pobee, "Perspectives for Ecumenical Formation Tomorrow," *The Ecumenical Review* 48, no. 4 (1996): 488.

44. Joint Working Group, "Ecumenical Formation," no. 1, 490.

45. Ibid., no. 15, 493.

46. De Santa Ana, "Research and Ecumenical Formation," 502, 503.

47. Pontifical Council for Promoting Christian Unity, *Directory for the Application*, no. 63.

48. Joint Working Group, "Ecumenical Formation," no. 15, 493.

49. Ibid., no. 26, 494.

CHAPTER 8

1. Kinnamon, *Can a Renewal Movement Be Renewed?* 153, 154 (see chap. 6, n. 14).

2. Kasper, *That They All May Be One*, 156 (see chap. 2, n. 13).

3. Ibid., 60.

4. Ibid., 170, 171, 172.

5. W. A. Visser 't Hooft, ed., *The Evanston Report: The Second Assembly of the World Council of Churches* (London: SCM Press, 1955), 91.

6. Bernard de Margerie, *In God's Reconciling Grace: Prayer and Reflection Texts for Christian Reconciliation and Unity* (Saskatoon, SK: The Roman Catholic Diocese of Saskatoon, 2014). This excellent resource contains a collection of prayers for both personal and congregational use, as well as ecumenical services/liturgies to promote interdenominational community prayer especially at the local level.

7. Ecumenical Meeting, 20th World Youth Day, August 19, 2005, as cited in *The Word Among Us* (May 2008): 26.

8. Carol Glatz, "Pope Skips Bishops Synod to Talk on Christian Unity," *The Prairie Messenger*, October 15, 2014, 2.

9. More information on each of these themes is available at http://www.tomryancsp.org/retreats.htm.

10. More information on Gospel Call is available at http://www.tomryancsp.org/gospelcall.htm.

11. Avis, *Reshaping Ecumenical Theology* 187, 188 (see chap. 1, n. 8).

12. Kasper, *Harvesting the Fruits*, 6 (see chap. 3, n. 6).

13. Ibid., 8.

14. Paul D. Murray, "Introducing Receptive Ecumenism," *The Ecumenist* 51, no. 2 (Spring 2014): 2, 3.

15. Kiply Lukan Yaworski, "Receptive Ecumenism: Practical, Flexible and Broad," *The Prairie Messenger*, January 1, 2014.

16. Paul D. Murray, "Establishing the Agenda," in *Receptive Ecumenism and the Call to Catholic Learning*, ed. Paul Murray (Oxford, UK: Oxford University Press, 2008), 16.

17. Ibid., 17.

18. Ibid., 17, 18.

19. Ibid., 15.

20. Yaworski, "Receptive Ecumenism."

21. Murray, "Introducing Receptive Ecumenism," 4.

22. Ibid.

23. Ibid., 4, 6.

24. Catherine Clifford, "50th Anniversary of the Decree on Ecumenism" (talk given, Toronto, Ontario, October 6, 2014).

25. Pope Francis, Apostolic Exhortation on the Joy of the Gospel (*Evangelii Gaudium*), November 2013, no. 246, http://www.vatican.va/evangelii-gaudium/en/.

26. Ibid.

27. Murray, "Introducing Receptive Ecumenism," 7.

28. Murray, "Establishing the Agenda," 11, 12.

29. Diane Kessler, "Ecumenical Spirituality: the Quest for Wholeness of Vision," in *The Vision of Christian Unity: Essays in Honor of Paul A. Crow, Jr.*, ed. Thomas F. Best and Theodore J. Nottingham (Indianapolis: Oikoumene Publications, 1997), 100.

30. Pope John Paul II, Apostolic Letter, *Novo Millennio Ineunte*, "At the Beginning of a New Millennium," January 6, 2001, no. 48, http://w2.vatican.va/content/john-paul-ii/en/apost_letters/2001/documents/hf_jp-ii_apl_20010106_novo-millennio-ineunte.html.

31. Ibid., no. 43.

CHAPTER 9

1. Dogmatic Constitution on the Church (*Lumen Gentium*), November 21, 1964, no. 23, http://www.vatican.va/archive/hist_councils/ii_vatican_council/documents/vat-ii_const_19641121_lumen-gentium_en.html; Decree on the Catholic Eastern Churches (*Orientalium Ecclesiarum*), November 21, 1964, no. 3, http://www.vatican.va/archive/hist_councils/ii_vatican_council/documents/vat-ii_decree_19641121_orientalium-ecclesiarum_en.html.

2. Catherine Clifford, "Journeying Together: Ecumenism in the 21st Century," *One in Christ* 48, no. 4 (2014): 12.

3. Canadian Conference of Catholic Bishops, "A Church in Dialogue," 18 (see chap. 1, n. 21).

4. The material in this section was in large measure first published in Thomas Ryan, "Ecumenical Spirituality for the Third Millennium," *One in Christ* 39, no. 2 (2004): 17–27. It is used with permission.

5. I am indebted in this section to Diane Kessler's article "The Forms of Protestant Spirituality: Reclaiming Our Roots," *Ecumenism* 116 (December 1994): 30–35.

6. Pew Forum on Religion and Public Life, *Global Christianity: A Report on the Size and Distribution of the World's Christian Population*, December 19, 2011, 67, http://www.pewforum.org/files/2011/12/Christianity-fullreport-web.pdf.

7. See paragraphs 27 and 31 on the Eucharist in World Council of Churches, "Baptism, Eucharist, and Ministry" (see chap. 2, n. 17).

8. Thomas Ryan, "Rejoicing in Our Differences," *Ecumenism* 92 (December 1988): 5.

9. Kessler, "Ecumenical Spirituality," 97, 98 (see chap. 8, n. 29).

10. See my book *A Survival Guide for Ecumenically Minded Christians* (Collegeville, MN: Liturgical Press, 1989), 113–15.

11. Margaret O'Gara, "The Theological Significance of Friendship in the Ecumenical Movement," in *That the World May Believe: Essays on Mission and Unity in Honour of George Vandervelde*, ed. Michael W. Goheen and Margaret O'Gara (Lanham, MD: University Press of America, 2005), 127–31.

CONCLUSION

1. Carl E. Braaten and Robert W. Jensen, eds. *In One Body through the Cross: The Princeton Proposal for Christian Unity* (Grand Rapids, MI: Eerdmans, 2003), no. 5.

2. International Anglican-Roman Catholic Commission for Unity and Mission, *Growing Together in Unity and Mission*, 2007, no. 7, http://www.vatican.va/roman_curia/pontifical_councils/chrstuni/angl-comm-docs/rc_pc_chrstuni_doc_20070914_growing-together_en.html.

3. World Council of Churches, *The Church*, no. 1 (see chap. 1, n. 7).

4. Prayer of the Fifth World Conference of Faith and Order, 1993.